The Spirit of Retirement

To Mark —
It's never too early
to plan the rest of your
life

Jim Renton

Also by James A. Autry

Books

The Servant Leader: How to Build a Creative Team, Develop Great Morale, and Improve Bottom-Line Performance

Love and Profit: The Art of Caring Leadership

Life & Work: A Manager's Search for Meaning

Confessions of an Accidental Businessman

Real Power: Business Lessons from the Tao Te Ching (with Stephen Mitchell)

Nights Under a Tin Roof (poetry)

Life After Mississippi (poetry)

Videos

Love & Profit

Life & Work

The Spirit At Work

(Available from Starthrower 1-800-242-3220 or www.starthrower.com)

THE
SPIRIT OF
RETIREMENT

Creating a Life of Meaning
and Personal Growth

JAMES A. AUTRY

Prima Publishing

Published by Prima Publishing, Roseville, California. Member of the Crown Publishing Group, a division of Random House, Inc., New York.

PRIMA PUBLISHING and colophon are trademarks of Random House, Inc., registered with the United States Patent and Trademark Office.

All products mentioned in this book are trademarks of their respective companies.

Library of Congress Cataloging-in-Publication Data
Autry, James A.
    The spirit of retirement : creating a life of meaning and personal growth /
James A. Autry.
        p.   cm.
    Includes index.
    ISBN 0-7615-6353-9
    1. Retirement—Psychological aspects. 2. Self-actualization (Psychology).
3. Maturation (Psychology).   4. Altruism. 5. Caring. 6. Retirees—Conduct of
life. I. Title.
HQ1062 .126.A87   2002
646.7'9—dc21   2002072500

03 04 05 06 HH 10 9 8 7 6 5 4 3 2
Printed in the United States of America

First Edition

Visit us online at www.primapublishing.com

Contents

To Norman Lear,
who in twenty-two years of friendship
has inspired me with his commitment to
family, friends, community,
and the life of service, meaning, and spiritual growth.

We must be willing to get rid of the life
we've planned, so as to have the life that
is waiting for us.

—*Joseph Campbell*

Acknowledgments

FULL DISCLOSURE: I confess that this book was not my idea. I'm just the person who wrote it.

It began when my editor, Alice Feinstein, called one day and said, "I have an idea for a book and I think you're just the author to write it. The subject is 'spiritual retirement planning.'"

It was one of those ideas that is so good you'd think someone would have already written such a book. But while there seemed to be jillions of books about financial planning for retirement, there were none about planning a life beyond leisure, recreation, and economic security.

So thank you, Alice, for the good idea, for allowing me to write it, and for then applying your usual keen eye and sharp ear to help make the manuscript better than it would have been.

Next I must acknowledge and thank my associate, Angela Renkoski, who not only juggles my schedule but who also did marathon work in researching and verifying the various Web sites and other references in this book, as well as contributing her ideas and comments on the manuscript itself.

I also thank my wife, Sally Pederson, and son Ronald, who had to put up with far too much of my angst as the deadline came closer and closer.

Finally, I offer my heartfelt thanks to all the people who allowed me to interview them and especially to those who let me tell their stories or quote them. What they have done, and are doing, in their lives has been an inspiration to me. Although I've not met all of these folks face-to-face, I still feel a deep personal connection with them, and my dream is to get them all together some day to introduce them to one another, and then have a big party (let's hope for a bestseller). They are, in alphabetical order:

Lex Alexander, Pat Barrentine, Joe Brownell, Carol Burns, Jeanne Cahill, John and Holly Clark, Jeanna Collins, Ray and Martha Lynn Crawford, Margie Daly, Betty Elliott, Julie Gammack, Sam Gore, Tom Gould, Mark Haverland, Elizabeth Hawkins, Bert Hill, David Jordan, Mike Kee, Spencer Longshore III, Ken and Peg McDougall, Don Mitchell, Adrienne Moen, Tracy Morris, Arthur Neis, Rev. James Newby, Hal Northrop, Brice Oakley and the ROC (Reinventing Our Careers) group, my father-in-law Gerald Pederson, Rick Prill, Josie RavenWing, Roy and Marilyn Reese, Kay Riley, Peter Roy, Drake Sadler, Tom Sawner, Marti Sivi, Terry Slinde, Cheryl Sypal, Virginia Traxler, Norman Van Klompenburg, Roberta Yoder, and JoAnn Zimmerman. Thanks, folks; I couldn't have done it without you.

Last and perhaps most important of all, thank you, reader, for buying this book.

Introduction

TIME HANGS LIKE a curse or a blessing over retirement. Which it's going to be for you depends on whether you let time liberate you—or enslave you.

We become enslaved when we are preoccupied with how things used to be, whom we used to know, what we used to do, where we used to go.

We are enslaved by memory when we feel that everything that's gone before is lost, never to be regained, like part of us is missing.

We are enslaved when, facing God's big deadline, we begin to think of ourselves and refer to ourselves as old and focus our attention on the physical activities our bodies no longer let us do.

We are liberated when we see ourselves as an accumulation of all the experiences, bad and good, we've ever had, all the people we've ever known, all the things we've ever done—and when we see that none of it is lost but rather has been part of the great adventure that nurtured us into who we are today.

We are liberated when we accept the infirmities of aging while maintaining the attitude that, in Gertrude Stein's words, "we are always the same age inside," and that we can imbue our lives with even more meaning now than ever before. On the surface, it's easy enough to intellectualize this attitude, but it's something else again to embrace with our minds and spirits the full potential of the rest of our lives.

In interviewing people for this book, I heard one comment so often I began to feel it must be typical of people who are about fifty years old. Again and again, they referred to the "second half" of their lives. It's the big joke: there are "half-time" parties, people talk about being on the "downhill" side, and so on.

Clearly, age fifty is not the halfway point; it's the two-thirds point for most people. So why the focus on midpoint? Easy enough to explain: It's our human attempt at lightheartedness, even bravado, in the face of inevitable aging and death.

There's another way to approach it, however, and that is to realize that, symbolically, we have indeed reached only the halfway point at fifty, or perhaps even older. If we choose the attitude of liberation about the rest of our lives, then *it is altogether possible that the final one-third of life can be as rich and full and as emotionally and spiritually rewarding as the first two-thirds*, perhaps more so.

The people whose stories appear in this book are inspiring examples of that attitude. In several cases, they chose liberation despite episodes of serious illness and disability. When I first began to look for these stories, I had the idea that I could create a list of categories that would serve as chapter titles, then I'd be able to find people whose stories fit the categories.

It has turned out that most of the people who are involved in one activity or interest or area of personal growth are involved also in others. I should have known. After all, it would be impossible to fit my own story into one of those arbitrary categories. I do a little bit of almost all of them.

In fact, my life since retirement has been so rich and fulfilling that I've come to feel that everything I've ever done has conspired to bring me to where I am now. But until very recent years, I did not seriously consider how this phase of life would be. I grew up without any concept whatsoever of retirement.

I come from farm people and country preachers, and I'm not sure I ever heard the word *retirement* before I went away to college. Old Mr. So-and-So might have become "too old to work," as it was said. And in every community there were a few of those "old folks" who generally spent their days sitting and, when visitors came, telling stories of the old days. But no one called it retirement.

So I entered the world of work never expecting to retire, only to find myself taking early retirement eleven years ago.

As long as I can remember, I've wanted to be an author, but because other things, mainly my career, kept interfering, my first book—written in my "spare time"—wasn't published until I was fifty. Now in retirement, I write almost every day. There has been one surprise, however, and that is writers not only write, they speak. So I find myself speaking to all kinds of groups, profit and nonprofit, secular and religious, seasoned professionals and students.

The most rewarding thing I can think of is to be published, to be read, and then to be invited to personally share my experiences and insights. Beyond those rewards are the ones that come from my coaching and counseling of executives and managers, as well as the conflict mediation and resolution I have regularly been called upon to do. I've also counseled and advised people about career changes and retirement.

All these experiences—speaking, coaching, counseling, advising, and writing—have led in one way or another to what I offer on these pages. In writing this book, I hope simply to share with you the thoughts, observations, advice, and information I've shared face-to-face over the past several years with many clients, colleagues, and friends.

In addition, I think you'll be inspired by the wonderful, exemplary stories I've chosen of people who are shining examples of an attitude of liberation. Their stories, along with the information and reference material in each chapter, are intended to help in your own journey toward retirement or, if you've already retired, to help you imbue your life with meaning, purpose, and personal and spiritual growth.

PART ONE

Preparing
for the
Big Transition

RETIREMENT PARTY

They all come,

even the ones who think

he was a pain in the neck.

They come and talk

about how he will be missed,

most of them never noticing he was there.

They come for themselves,

like going to a funeral

out of the fear of being buried alone someday.

They line up for coffee

and punch and cookies,

there being no official alcohol on the premises.

They read telegrams from old customers and old vendors

1

and old office buddies long retired.
They give him the right gift,
the rod and reel
or the camp stove
or the camera
or the round-trip ticket to somewhere,
bought with the fives and ones and quarters
from the manila envelope that has
in his last month
made its way all around the company.

He is moved by the attention,
by the feeling he is loved
and will be missed
and things won't be the same without him,
and he says some words
about how he will never forget any of them.
He introduces his family who came halfway
   across the country
just for the occasion,
then everybody drifts toward their offices
saying good-bye with things like
"You lucky bastard,"
and "You don't even have to get up tomorrow,"
and "Stay in touch,"
and "Come visit,"
and other words of comfort for times like these.

                —From *Love and Profit*, James A. Autry, 1991

RETIREMENT FROM ANY kind of American organization, profit or nonprofit, has developed its own mythology accompanied by rituals and communal observances that are not unlike a funeral. Too often, the net effect on the retiree has been a self-perception somewhere between has-been and never-was.

It doesn't have to be that way. Instead, retirement can become a liberating path toward a life of opportunity along with personal and spiritual growth. But you have to want it, which means you have to accept and embrace a way of thinking that will move you positively through the transition. It begins with aligning your own perceptions and intentions with the new reality of your life.

To help with the transition, the beginning section of this book offers three "macro" chapters that provide an overview of observations and advice about adjusting your attitude, followed by a list of questions in chapter 2 to help you focus on how to let go of the old and embrace the new. Chapter 3 then examines the factors that help define a life of meaning and spiritual growth.

You'll also find personal stories interspersed between these chapters, as indeed you will discover them throughout the book. The stories share experiences and insights of other people who have gone through, or are going through, the process of planning a retirement life of meaning and growth. The themes and ideas within these stories are intended to help you as much as possible in your own journey.

CHAPTER ONE

Adjusting Your Attitude

UNDERSTAND THIS: THERE can be a terrible loss of identity when you retire. If you have defined yourself by what you do—and most of us have defined ourselves that way at one point or another—then when what you do goes away, so does a large part of the person you perceive yourself to be.

I've seen it many times. A person retires, and there's the retirement party, the celebration, the gifts, the good wishes, and that happy morning when he or she doesn't have to get up and go to work. But after the vacation and the golf games and fishing excursions and the long-postponed household projects, the reality hits and hits hard: "I don't have a job. For the first time in my life I don't have a job."

Then one day he or she decides to just drop by the office to see how things are, to chat up some old colleagues, maybe to have lunch in the company cafeteria or in one of the old midday watering holes frequented by everyone "in the business."

It is one of the saddest sights at any company: the recent retiree making the rounds, dropping in for a chat, completely unaware that he or she is now an interruption to the person who is politely smiling and nodding.

Why do people get into this situation? Why do they feel the need to return to the workplace, as if connected by some emotional or psychological umbilical cord? Why can't they cut loose? Simple. Even though they think they have planned comprehensively for retirement, they are nevertheless suffering from a lack of the right kind of planning.

"We should remember," consultant Roberta Yoder says, "that 'retirement' is an economic term, not a social, psychological, emotional, or spiritual term. Thus it really applies only to the economic, or work, phase of life."

Her friend, Adrienne Moen, expands the thought: "People should try to think about other ways to spell *retirement*. How about *transition, change, another season, a passage*, and so on?"

It's fruitless as well as depressing to try to keep up with what's happening at the old workplace. If there are friendships, of course they should continue to be nurtured, but only in social settings away from the office.

6

Beyond that, realize that retirement is the time to move on, the time to make that new start so many of us dream about. In fact, retirement is the grand opportunity to stop *doing* and concentrate on *being*, to become the person you want to be.

YOU CAN INITIATE this process, of course, after you retire, but it's much better to start while still active in your work life. You begin with some realistic understandings about time.

Most professional people feel that, though they may be busy twelve or sixteen hours a day, they essentially are in control of their own time.

> *Retirement is the time to move on, the time to make that new start so many of us dream about.*

"That's nonsense," says Hal Northrop, retired CEO of Callaway Gardens, whose considerable management experience includes service on several public company boards. "Most people in organizations have not been responsible for their own schedules. Most often, circumstances have dictated where they spend their time. They've been reacting most of the time during these years and haven't realized it. The result is that a lot of people face retirement not knowing how to use their time because, most often, how they use their time has been determined for them. They just haven't realized it."

Jeanna Collins (see her story, page 233) admits that the change in the structure of her day caused some problems in using her time efficiently. "Regardless of your mind-set," she says, "you don't just walk away from thirty-four years of a certain way of life and not expect to go through some times of doubt, questioning, fear, lack of confidence, lack of feeling useful, realization of your life coming to an end, and so on."

Jeanna suspects a lot of newly retired people have these feelings, and she warns that they can lead to a point of doing less and less instead of more and more. "It can put you in a funk."

Northrop puts an inordinate emphasis on time when advising others about retirement planning. "I believe that how people use their time after retirement," he says, "is the major ingredient in their longevity.

"Not only that," he continues, "but how we physically and mentally use our time is a measure of our true character, of what we're made of, because it takes discipline and character to use that time for continued personal and spiritual growth. I've seen too many people become sedentary, overeat, become overweight, develop health problems and die, because they didn't know how to use their time to create or continue a life of growth—or they didn't develop the discipline to do it."

IF YOU'RE LIKE most people, and particularly if you're a baby boomer, you probably feel you already put much time and effort into retirement planning, but have you planned your *life* or only your income? Have you considered the emotional and spiritual, rather than just the financial, aspects of retirement?

An entire category of media—books, magazines, advertisements by the hundreds—is devoted to promoting one financial planning service or another. Their illustrations feature the ubiquitous AARP (formerly known as the American Association of Retired Persons) couple: a handsome, silver-haired man, lean, trim, tanned, and fit, paired with an equally youthful-looking silver-haired woman. These beautiful people with movie star teeth are always smiling as they ski or swim or fish or golf or gaze from the deck of a luxury liner. And the message is always the same: Our financial planners or investment counselors or mutual fund managers or securities brokers can help you find that feeling of well-being, contentment, and security that will allow you to have the fullest possible retirement. Well-being. Contentment. Security.

Add to these scenarios the same beautiful couple dancing romantically across a page featuring a promotion for Viagra, and the inevitable conclusion is that the retiring baby boomers will want for absolutely nothing.

Except what, perhaps?

The answer begs a definition of well-being, contentment, and security. Does it include emotional fulfillment, joy, and bliss? Does it include a deep sense of connection with the people you most care about and who most care about you? And what about a continuing or a renewed quest for a greater understanding of the ageless mysteries, of the great unknown, of a higher power, of God?

The media induce you to look forward to the good life. Nothing wrong with that. But this book asks you to go beyond the good life and consider also the life of goodness.

When you plan the financial aspects of retirement, you don't just put the money away and forget about it. You pay attention to what's happening with it; you actively manage it, working that into your daily or weekly schedule. You must do the same thing with your spiritual retirement planning. You can't just say, "When I retire, I'll take time for the things that enrich my inner life." You have to take time now and begin to practice those things now. Just as there should be a seamless transition in your financial life, there should be an equally seamless transition in your spiritual life.

Retired Colonel Tom Sawner (see his story, page 13), a former jet fighter pilot who was once the Air Force's Top Gun, says, "A lot of folks spend a lot of retirement time figuring out what's next. They would feel more fulfilled if they started that quest earlier." Then he adds, "It's not true that nobody likes change but a wet baby; nobody likes change until it becomes more uncomfortable not to change. When they understand that discomfort, that's when the quest for meaning begins. Better that it happen sooner than later."

Jeanne Cahill (see her story, page 208), who owned and ran a successful exercise equipment company, says she started early: "There was no formal planning but instead a period of introspection. What did I want to do that work had prevented? . . . What was my passion? I made lists of things that seemed important, then I added to and subtracted from the list as time went on. Three things I knew: I wanted plenty of time for contemplation. I knew I would do things to benefit others while giving me a sense of purpose. And I would maintain my good health because I knew a healthy inner life is more possible with a healthy physical life."

In thinking about planning for a life of meaning and purpose and spiritual growth, there are lessons we in the West could learn from Eastern religions, particularly some of those practiced in India. To one extent or another, the devout generally embrace three basic phases of religious and spiritual life. The first two are student and householder, then, in the third, the householder gives it all up, gets a bowl, takes to the streets and countryside, begs for his food, and lives the life of a hermit in order to diligently pursue a higher spiritual level.

To our Western minds this approach is too extreme, and in fact only a small percentage of believers fully engage in this third phase; nonetheless, this example is useful in helping you think about retirement as a time of life that can have greater spiritual content and meaning and that can put more emphasis on pursuits other than the comforts and pleasures that characterize the popular notion of a good life.

Thus, the objective of spiritual retirement planning should be to arrive at retirement day with an absolute, deep belief that life so far has been just a prelude to *now*, that it has all been part of making you who you are today so that you can concentrate less on the doing and more on the being, less on yourself and more on others. Next is the realization that everything that has gone before adds up to a you who is ready to make a difference in something other than product or process or profit. You can say, "I've done that and I've done it well, but it was not who I am, only what I did. Now I can concentrate on who I am and discover a person who is more than the sum of a thirty-year career."

This book will help in your journey toward a retirement of meaning in two ways: by telling other people's stories of their own retirement journey, including the difficulties as well as the successes, and by offering ideas and suggestions for the kinds of opportunities and endeavors available for your investigation and pursuit. You may choose one, you may select several ideas, or you may simply create your own path after considering those offered here.

Just remember that, while you may indeed choose to do works of significance and you may make admirable accomplishments on your retirement path, these choices are not about accomplishment or recognition or reward; they are only about being and becoming who you want to be for the rest of your life.

TOM'S STORY

A Brush with Death
Clarifies the Priorities

Several years ago, Lieutenant Colonel Tom Sawner, now retired, was living the perfect dream of a fighter pilot: He was not only soon-to-be commander of a squadron of F-16s, the world's best fighter plane, but he was also the Air Force's Top Gun. "I was doing neat and wonderful stuff by anyone's definition, including my own," he says. Then Hurricane Andrew blew it all away.

But the hurricane was not really the culprit; it was only the catalyst of a deeper, more personal experience. "It wasn't exactly a road-to-Damascus kind of experience," says Tom, "but it was very similar because I was in a place where I thought I was going to die every three minutes for six hours."

It's not that Tom hadn't prepared for the storm, done everything he could do to be ready. He had. "I've been a Boy Scout for over thirty years, so I was prepared. We had stockpiled water, spare batteries, fuel for the stove, lanterns and generator, nonperishable food. I had covered every door and window with heavy plywood." All this after flying back into Miami on the last airline flight to land prior to the storm.

Tom and his wife had been called for a last-minute and final deathbed visit to his father-in-law in New England. The hurricane was not predicted to arrive until later in the week, but as the Sawners were to return, they discovered that the storm was moving in and that their children had been evacuated to Tampa by the nanny and the neighbors. So Tom's wife diverted to Tampa on one airliner while he flew back on another to prepare the house.

By the time the house had been protected, it was too late for him to escape. "Besides," as he explains, "I was ten feet tall and bulletproof. I had been through four other hurricanes, and this one was only forecast to be a category 3 storm. But apparently no one told that to Mother Nature. The storm was a category 5, and our street got hit with a microtornado that was embedded in the storm. We lost power fairly early on that Sunday night, but I had a small transistor radio. As the storm grew, the plywood on the windows and doors started to break. The storm came into the house, almost like a living thing. I kept retreating from one fortified area to the next, as it almost seemed to chase me through the house. Each new room I retreated into was destroyed. Finally, I was in the closet of the last undamaged room on the lee side of the house from the storm, just me and our pet bird and pet gerbil, huddled in the closet. Shortly after I got in the closet and as the roof was coming off, I distinctly remember hearing the radio announcer say that the worst would hit in about an hour.

"Even though I had prepared for the worst I thought the hurricane could do," he says, "at that moment I knew that after all my preparations I wasn't going to survive."

Within the furor of the storm came a moment of calm insight. "I had thought my life was good; I had an apparently good marriage, great kids. My head was okay, but I realized that my heart was heavy, and I didn't know why exactly. I started asking myself, 'Have I done everything that I can?' I ended up with tremendous clarity because everything that usually tugs at my mind was gone; it seemed that I had incredible mental power, so I asked myself, 'Why not use this time?'"

Tom started by asking himself what he regretted. At first he thought, "Nothing." Then, he says, "Out of left field came this thought: My regret is that I'm not going to get to see my kids grow up. But where did that come from? I've been there for them, had all the insurance, the educational savings. Their mother was a good person and would be with them. But it came to me that my regret was not only that I was not going to be there to see them grow up, but, more important, I was not going to get to model the kind of person I wanted them to be."

This was a profound insight for Tom, but one he thought he'd never have the opportunity to act on. Then the storm died down.

Tom's first reaction was, "'Oh, shit, I'm going to live after all. Now I'm going to have to deal with all this stuff.'

"The more I went back to that time in the storm, the time I'd been in that different place psychologically, the more I asked myself, 'If I want this meaning in my life, if

I want this with the kids, then why am I working twelve to fourteen hours a day?'"

Tom, like many busy, hardworking parents, had convinced himself that he was doing it "for the kids." His moment of clarity revealed the fallacy of that assumption, so he made big changes in his life.

"It's not true," he says, "that nobody likes change but a wet baby. Nobody likes change until it becomes more uncomfortable not to change. When they understand that discomfort, that's when the quest for meaning begins."

Tom resigned from the Air Force and took a position with the Air National Guard, not flying airplanes but still doing good and worthwhile work in leadership training.

He and his wife of fifteen years realized that their lives would be better off if they ended their marriage, so they were divorced. Tom, with custody of his children, was on his way to a new life, one of more connection with his family, particularly his children, and a life of more meaning. "The lesson," he says, "is to look for good things within the things you think are bad. As it turned out, the experience in the storm was good for my life."

After starting his work with the Air National Guard, Tom's life seemed back on track. Everything seemed to be going well, a new house, the kids with him, and a wonderful lady in his life, but this is not to be the happy ending. The following year Tom was diagnosed with lymphatic cancer. After major surgery and two rounds of radiation, the cancer was "cured."

"The hurricane helped me understand what was really important, and I had time to realign my life," Tom says. "I'm convinced that without the changes I made and the support and love from Bettina [his fiancée], I would not have been able to survive the cancer. That was the gift from the hurricane to me."

Four months after the final radiation treatment, Tom and Bettina married, and it seemed all was back on track; however, once again, it was not to be. At his twelve-month checkup, the CT scan discovered more cancer. This time it was worse, and extensive chemotherapy was the treatment.

Once again Tom was a survivor, and once again he learned new lessons. "In my chemotherapy-induced inactivity, I knew that my very life could depend on looking ahead with an attitude of optimism. Viktor Frankel said that the people who live longer are those who still have something left to do with their lives. So I decided I'd damn well better have lots left to do in my life."

As he says, "You would be amazed how much planning you can do with five to six hours of chemo-induced insomnia every night for eight months." So lying there, he made plans for a life after his medical retirement from the Air National Guard. He planned a lodge he calls River Oak. "I 'walked' every room in the lodge at least a thousand times. Each night I would focus on a different room and work out the layout and solve any problems with it.

"Retirement must be thought of as a significant emotional event," he says. "Suddenly you can't define your life through the work you do. It would be better if people started planning earlier, but it's never too late to seek a life of meaning. The reason I think so many retirees return to their workplace to visit is that they are drawn to return to the scene of the meaning. But the meaning must now be found elsewhere."

After he beat cancer the first time, Tom began to keep a journal on his computer of musings and observations. He has turned these entries into a presentation he calls "Life Lessons of a Cancer Survivor," which he now does as a volunteer service at cancer centers. And he has launched his next career, but he will never return to the grind, and he will always have time for those he loves.

> *"Build things before you need them. Build relationships before you need them. Build meaning before you need it. Build for retirement before you need it."*

"One of my most important 'cancer' thoughts is that time not spent with those you love is *not* time postponed; it is time *lost*. There are many lessons I've learned. Among them are that you have to build things before you need them. Build relationships before you need them. Build meaning before you need it. Build for retirement before you need it."

I asked Tom whether, out of all his experiences and close calls in airplanes, in the storm, and in the hospital bed, he had thoughts on spirituality he'd like to share with others. At first, he seemed reluctant and said, "Let me think about it." Then he e-mailed me the following, which I present with virtually no editing:

> Spirituality is the individual belief that there is a higher meaning and a greater responsibility than the physical day-to-day existence that we lead. I believe the head is the center of the intellect and the origin of rational behavior: Think of it as the "doing" part; the body is the center of physical response and the origin of sexual behavior: the "feeling" part; and the heart is the center of emotional response and the origin of empathetic behavior: the "caring" part. Spirituality is the intersection between head, body, and heart. Spirituality is the tug between what your brain is telling you will provide the best advantage, what your body wants to feel, and what you know in your heart is "right."

> Spirituality is often found in the triumph of long-term good over . . . short-term gain. Spirituality is how personal values manifest themselves in actual daily living, the actions that we take and the choices that we make. Spirituality is not something that just happens; it must be built and nurtured. Spirituality requires introspection and is often the result of a search for meaning. Spirituality is what gives strength in times of trouble and the belief that there is good even in the bad. Spirituality often comes out of adversity, like good steel forged in the hottest fire.

Spirituality is often connected to religion, but is less about faith and more about righteousness, less about a specific belief and more about a higher calling. I feel especially spiritual when I do what I know is right even when, and most especially when, I know no one else will ever know of my choice or my action. To me it is to teach, to mentor, to coach, to assist, to "help," without any compensation or thought of reward other than knowing the world will be a better place because of my action. . . .

Spirituality is about relationships, relationships with others, but especially the relationship you have with yourself. Each of us continuously has a myriad of competing values within our self. . . . Our ability to care about others and to value being cared about, our ability to value ourselves and to know what is right is being spiritual.

Spirituality is also about respect for life. I believe all life, from the smallest microbe to the most complex human, has purpose and adds meaning to our existence. Therefore, it is inappropriate to judge that one is more or less important than any other. While I am certainly not a pacifist or vegetarian, any taking of life, whether plant, animal, or human, must be done deliberately and with conscious thought because, once done, it cannot be undone. . . .

It's no surprise that I feel most spiritual when I have the opportunity to sit or walk for an extended time in the woods. The ability to clear the mind without the intrusions of normal life allows me clarity, a sense of linkage, and an almost physical feeling of connection with a universal life force, distinct from any specific thing, but connected to all. To me, this is the most spiritual time of all.

CHAPTER TWO

Learning to Let Go

NO ONE INTERVIEWED for this book believes that the transition to retirement is easy. It requires discipline, focus, and hard work, not to mention a large dose of honest introspection.

Introspection is not just something you one day decide to have. You can't develop it overnight, and some people never get it. They never examine their own lives, and they never see themselves as others see them. Plato's observation that "the life which is unexamined is not worth living" is probably too harsh, but it is true that the unexamined life is likely to be one without significant personal or spiritual growth.

There are no formulas for introspection and reflection, but in helping you begin to look inside yourself, to examine your attitudes and preconceptions, and to take the next steps in preparing yourself for retirement, I offer the following questions. They are in two somewhat arbitrary categories that I'll call the "thinking/doing questions" and the "feeling/being questions." Both categories contain questions for those of you who are contemplating and planning retirement as well as for those of you who are already retired but who still feel there are aspects to retirement life you'd like to reexamine and, perhaps, adjust or change. In addition, on page 28, I have included a set of questions specifically for those who have already retired.

> *The unexamined life is likely to be one without significant personal or spiritual growth.*

The answers to all these questions will require—in addition to discipline, focus, and hard work—considerable time for reflection as well as complete honesty with yourself, plus one other thing: imagination. The good news is that you already have most of the answers deep within you. To paraphrase the poet Percy Bysshe Shelley, you have but to learn to imagine what you already know.

The "Thinking/Doing" Questions

1. When you think of the word *retirement*, what image comes to mind? Is it an old or aging person? If so, what is

he or she doing? Puttering around the house? Playing golf, fishing? How then do you think you will fit that image? Do you see yourself differently? Why?

2. Are you looking forward to retirement? If so, why? What is it about retirement you are positively anticipating? Make a list.

3. How do you describe yourself, by who you are or by what you do? How much of who you perceive yourself to be is defined by what you do? A good test is to observe how you most often introduce yourself. Do you feel compelled, within the first few minutes, to tell what your position or job is?

4. When you meet other people, are you more interested in what they do or who they are? Do you distinguish between the two?

5. When you think of yourself in retirement, do you think of it in terms of what you are going to *do* next? If so, you first need to identify and accept that you're *not* going to do the same things you've been doing.

6. What are you dreading about retirement, if anything? Make a list.

7. Ask yourself how much you love just being at the workplace. Put aside all the clichés of how you're supposed to feel, or think you're supposed to feel, and ask yourself the honest question "How much will I miss just being there?" I retired about the same time as a friend and colleague who was one of my peers in the management group. About six months after our retirement, we

got together to catch up. I'd not been back in the old office building since my retirement party. He'd been back every week. "I just miss everything about it," he said, "the job, the people, even the damned building." His comments made me very sad for him yet happy that I'd been able to make such a clean break.

In answering this question, don't discount the everyday stuff such as lunches in the cafeteria or at the corner deli with your friends, or that coffee on your birthday when your colleagues gather briefly to give you funny cards and to joke about your age. You may miss Secretaries' Week (now called in some places "Administrative Assistants' Week") with the flowers and the candy, or picking your sports teams and putting a dollar in the office pool, or those times when a group of you organizes a charity event in the company. It is these kinds of activities and social concourse that help create the rich texture of your work life, and you must face the fact that you'll miss some of it.

8. List the things you like about the job itself that are going to go away. For me, I knew I'd miss being a leader in an industry and being respected for my accomplishments in that industry. I knew all that would be gone because I'd seen industry leaders retire and knew that they were out of sight, out of mind. I knew also that I'd miss being involved in creating new products and bringing them to market.

Betty Elliott, a retired receptionist and administrative assistant, told me that retirement has been a huge adjustment for her because she loved being with the people at work. "Not just my fellow workers," she says, "but the almost constant stream of interesting people who visited the company. It was my job to receive them and make sure they got to the right person or place. I must have met at least one new fascinating person a week."

9. Now list the things you don't like and that you'll be happy to leave behind. I was sick of the incessant pressure of earnings, the endless meetings, the constant travel, and simply having a boss.

Joe Brownell, a retail salesman in a clothing store, told me that he enjoys selling but that he'll be happy not to have a sales quota hanging over his head or being reminded about it by his boss every day. For Betty Elliott, it was the time clock. "And I hated rushing to make it to work on time. I don't miss that."

Try to evaluate how these things balance out. Try to determine the trade-offs that will be okay and the ones that will disturb you. Unless you identify what you'll miss and won't miss, you will not be able to process and deal with these issues. (As part of my preretirement process, I went to a psychotherapist for counseling.)

10. List the personal—not work—things that your job allows you to do, such as travel to nice resorts for conferences, maintain a circle of professional friends and contacts, perhaps be a member of a nice club, eat in good restaurants, and so on. Or your organization might be one of those that provides computers or other equip-

ment for personal use. In some cities, there's simple personal prestige in working for certain companies, and often employees of those companies receive courtesy discounts on everything from clothing to automotive supplies, or even discounts at restaurants and movies. Your job may entail many purely personal advantages; be sure to include them all.

11. Now list the personal things the job keeps you from doing, such as more time with family or with hobbies and interests. And don't forget about not having enough time for intellectual growth through learning new things, reading, taking courses, and so on. Not to mention the fact that you have only so much vacation time and that your travel must fit into an overall vacation schedule. Match these lists; evaluate the trade-offs.

The "Feeling/Being" Questions

While these answers will indeed require thought, the objective is to identify your honest emotional response. Don't come up with the answer you think you ought to give but the one that is closest to your feelings.

1. Make a list answering this question: What do I really value most in my life? The job, family, friends, activities? Then put them in priority order according to how you really feel about them (remember, not how you think you ought to feel). If the job is near the top of the

list, then at retirement, you'll be needing a major values shift.

2. How do you think you are going to feel (or how do you feel) about being replaced in your job, about not being considered relevant to the organization anymore, about now not having your opinion valued, about no longer being asked to make "important" decisions, about being "out of the loop" *forever?*

3. If no one knew what you had done in your professional life and knew you only for who you are, would that bother you? Would it be satisfying enough? Do you think they would like you or respect you to the same degree? Less? More?

4. If you would not be satisfied by people knowing you only for who you are, rather than for what you do or what position you hold, does that mean your sense of self is derived from what others think of you more than what you think of yourself? Be open to the possibility that your answer to this question might lead to a need for counseling or therapy.

5. Who would you like to be, and how would you like to be thought of ten years from now? Try to describe your ideal self ten years from now.

6. What do you think you'll miss, or what do you already miss, about being younger? What do you miss from your earlier life, perhaps even from childhood?

7. Whom would you want to see again, perhaps family or old friends, if you had the chance?

FOR THOSE WHO HAVE ALREADY RETIRED

1. What are you doing now that you had not planned to do? What are you not doing that you had planned to do? Comparing the two, explain to yourself what happened. Have you been disappointed? Is there a change you'd like to make?

2. What has been the biggest surprise of your retirement? Why?

3. Since retirement, have you managed to find time for things that you feel contribute to your personal and spiritual growth? If not, what's preventing it? Can you change those circumstances?

4. Do you still have things you look forward to every day?

5. Do you feel as useful as you did when you were working?

6. Do you have close friends? Would you like to have more close friends?

7. How has retirement affected the relationship between you and your spouse/partner?

8. Make a list of things you still want to do, see, or experience. Be expansive; give your imagination free reign. Don't be limited by considerations of money, health, or time. You can deal with those in the next step. In interviewing people for this book, I found that the most active and vibrant retirees were those

who were consistently open to the possibilities for new experiences, from going back to school to trekking in the wilderness.

9. Now write each of those things in answer 8 on a separate sheet of paper. In a column on the left side, list the factors preventing you from doing, seeing, or experiencing whatever it is. Here's where money, health, or time may enter the picture. In a column on the right side, list the factors that encourage or enable you. Compare the columns; determine whether the barriers are so insurmountable that you are not likely to overcome them. But be honest. Don't take the easy answer. As one of my publisher friends used to ask, "Is it impossible or merely inconvenient?" If it's merely inconvenient, then the barrier is not insurmountable. If, however, it is impossible, and if that's likely to be the case forever, throw this sheet away. If you're not sure and think there's even a possibility you could overcome the barriers someday, put the sheet in a "someday" pile. If there are no insurmountable barriers, then put the sheet in a "yes" pile. Move on to the next desired experience, and do the same thing. At the end of this exercise, you essentially have established for yourself an agenda of things that you want to do, see,

(continues)

or experience; not only that, you have identified the ones you can act on right now. The last step is to put them in some priority order. As Jeanne Cahill (see her story, page 208) says, "The best advice I can give to my fellow retired people is don't fall into the doldrums and keep putting off what you want to do. There'll never be a better time than right now to do whatever it is. As the ad says, 'Just do it.'"

8. What have you always wanted to do but never had the chance?

9. Whom do you really love?

10. With whom do you truly desire to spend more time?

11. Whom would you really like to help?

12. Whom do you really trust?

13. Why don't you trust more people?

14. Do you have true and abiding friendships or just acquaintances?

15. Do you have the emotional capacity to be alone, or do you always need people around you? (Being alone does *not* include watching television or surfing the Internet alone.)

16. List your talents and not just your skills.

17. How good are you at doing nothing?

18. Describe yourself in spiritual or, if you prefer, in religious terms. How important is this aspect to you?

19. Do you think of yourself has having a spiritual quest? Of being spiritually curious?

20. Do you pray or meditate? How do you feel about those things? Are they important to you or marginal in your life?

What Now?

The process of developing honest and deeply felt answers to all these questions may take weeks or even months of work. In addition, you'll find that your answers provoke other questions that need to be answered. For instance, if in the list of thinking/doing questions you are giving answers that indicate you're really going to miss being at the workplace more than you're looking forward to retirement, this is a danger signal and raises the question of what you're going to do about it.

Too often, we think that this is a bridge we can cross when we get to it. "Of course I'm going to miss the job and the people and the action," you might think, "but I'll find something else to take its place." What we fail to consider is that we didn't arrive at our jobs and in our positions overnight, and we won't be able to find that "something else" overnight, either.

In the feeling/being questions, if your answers indicate that you have acquaintances but not friends, if you can't identify people you love and want to be with, whether family or friends, this is an even larger danger signal. Most of us who have retired have been shocked by how fast those great folks we knew "in the business" simply faded from our radar screens, or vice versa. When you retire, the reason for those relationships often disappears. The frames of reference change, the subjects you once discussed are no longer relevant, and the bonds of professional association simply don't now exist.

The objective of the exercises in this chapter is to identify what you need to do now, whether one year or ten years from retirement—or for that matter already retired—to assure that you continue life as a whole person, not a shadow of who you were "on the job."

Much of the remainder of this book will examine ideas and stories of how to be ready and how to respond. These are told from the point of view of people who are successfully planning a retirement of personal and spiritual growth as well as retirees who are succeeding at it.

Here also are a few small tips that can help you begin the transition or, if you're already retired, can perhaps enrich or even help move you toward the next phase of your retirement life:

- If you've spent your work life dealing with people and being surrounded by people, learn to be alone. Spend time at it. Get comfortable with it. Again, being alone does not include watching television or surfing the Internet.

- If your job has involved working alone, then do the opposite: Learn to be with people. Volunteer in some group activity—civic, church, or otherwise.

- Do something different. Break the routine you now have and practice some things you might want to embrace in retirement (even though you may end up embracing different things when the time comes).

- If you've spent your professional life working with words and numbers in an office setting, start working with your hands. Garden. Build something, even something small like a birdhouse, squirrel feeder, or a single bookshelf.

- If your job has been physical, then put your mind to work in your off hours. Read. Attend good films or plays or concerts. Take a course in adult education or even a course on tape.

- Don't be afraid to get some psychological or spiritual counseling if you're having real problems dealing with some of these questions or answers. Just as you may have engaged a financial planner or counselor as part of your retirement planning, you should consider calling on professionals for the personal aspects of retirement as well. It could be the best investment you make for the rest of your life.

- Plan and have discussions with your spouse or partner. What are his or her expectations of retirement? The theologian and author Sam Keen is fond of quoting one of his mentors: "The two big questions in life are 'Where am I going?' and 'Who's going with me?'" How will your spouse or domestic partner's life be enhanced or disrupted by your choices? If the honest answers to these questions demonstrate that different paths are likely, this point should be understood ahead of time so that you can maintain a strong relationship while still being involved in separate interests or activities. Personal counseling may be appropriate here as well.

BY NOW YOU realize that the process of planning for a retirement of meaning and purpose, of seeking personal and spiritual growth, and of deepening connections within yourself and with others is no minor task. You can't add "spiritual retirement planning" to your weekend "to do" list and expect to whip through these questions and answers and then check them off, along with mowing the lawn and repairing the gutters and downspouts.

In fact, it is important to realize that answering these questions may lead you to no less than a complete realignment of how you choose to live your life from now on. The difficult truth is that if you can't find spiritual growth and fulfillment in your work, you'll have trouble finding it in your retirement. So much greater the reason for starting now. Because, you see, when all is said and done, when the work life ends, when the new future is at hand, how you have chosen to live your life, how you have set yourself to be the person you want to be, is the only answer that matters.

PAT'S STORY

Live as If You'll Never Retire

One of Pat Barrentine's favorite quotes is "If you want to make God laugh, tell her (or him) your plans."

Pat and her late husband, Gene, didn't really plan for retirement, not even financially. "We had more of a philosophy than a plan," she says. "Our married life began, I think fortunately, before the advent of credit cards. The only purchases we made using credit were our houses. Each month we set aside funds in a savings account and later also in IRAs and other investments."

As for planning a life of personal and spiritual growth after retirement, Pat explains, "My belief is that we create the quality of our retirement by choices made years earlier in how we live and what we value. It's so much more than what we might write down as a plan. Living well is a choice that follows clear intention and a lot of faith, not only in yourself but in something far greater and wiser."

She offers this comment to those who are looking toward a retirement life of meaning and growth: "The important question is 'What do you value?' If it's money, property, cars, trinkets, and other 'stuff,' you're not likely to develop a deep spiritual awareness simply because you stop working. But being spiritual does not also mean you can't be prosperous and live a good life. Poverty is not required. You're looking for deeper meaning and connection with your authentic self. It's a wonderful search. I think the main reason any of us is here is to explore and discover who we are and what we have to offer to the whole."

Like many other people interviewed for this book, Pat insists that a person can't just wait and decide to "do" spiritual and personal growth. "Spiritual isn't a 'doing'; it's a 'being,'" she says, adding, "Don't put off anything that's important to you, hoping to have time for it when you retire. If it's important, start now."

Pat says she learned this lesson both negatively and positively. "My father's belief was that he'd make his 'fortune' first and then have time for friends. Inevitably,

> *"I think the main reason any of us is here is to explore and discover who we are and what we have to offer to the whole."*

he did neither and died at age sixty-five. My husband's parents never fooled themselves that a postal worker was going to get financially rich. What mattered to them was a life of rich relationships with friends and family. They always had enough and celebrated their seventieth anniversary before their deaths. My lesson from them is that to be happy in life we must live what we value."

Gene and Pat were not traditionally "religious" people, yet they knew they needed to find some deeper meaning in their lives. "Taking Mind Dynamics . . . was the first of many explorations into 'new thought,' meta-physics, and spirituality," Pat explains. "Mind Dynamics taught limitless thinking—that we are connected to everything . . . that we are all part of God, whatever you want to call it. Once my husband and I touched the richness of exploration, it became a part of us and allowed us to see beyond appearances to embrace a larger possibility. . . . Our sons took the courses with us, adding to the richness of conversations at the dinner table. Gene and I started meditating together every evening."

One of the benefits of the spiritual journey that Gene and Pat shared was how it permeated everything they did together, from walking in the great outdoors, to bike riding, to playing tennis. It gave them a greater sensitivity to people and to organizations and causes that serve people. They treasured friendships with greater intensity, and they turned their vacation travels into extensions of their spiritual quest.

"Our choices for travel took us to natural places like the Amazon, Galapagos Islands, Tahiti, on a Barefoot Windjammer Cruise. Never did we seek out a big hotel on the beach. In Hawaii we stayed in Hilo at a little place back in the neighborhoods that had its own jungle in the backyard. We hiked through volcanoes and to the top of mountains, into botanical gardens, and waterfalls. Yosemite became our favorite place to celebrate our wedding anniversary, and on our thirty-second and thirty-fourth, we hiked to the top of Yosemite Falls."

When the time came to choose a place to retire, they sought someplace that was rural, slower paced, but still with affordable activities. "Finding the right place became an exploration," Pat says. "After a couple visits to senior developments in Arizona, we knew we didn't want to be totally surrounded by 'old people.' The many amenities were tempting, but we wanted diversity. We felt it was important to have friends of all ages. That easily eliminated several choices."

During what had been a gently paced exploration of retirement possibilities, Gene was diagnosed with multiple myeloma, bone marrow cancer, which made their search considerably more urgent. Also, the diagnosis meant that he would not be able to work the five additional years he had planned on, which meant less money set aside for retirement.

Pat still celebrates the travel adventures she and Gene shared before his diagnosis. "How fortunate that we had not put off those trips he most wanted to make—especially one to the Amazon jungle. So many adventures we had shared remained rich in our memory. Had we saved them for that 'someday' when we were retired, we could have lived instead with regret. Of course, after the diagnosis, we still traveled—to Tahoe, Santa Fe, Sedona, Monterey, and Carmel, but we just didn't fly anymore."

Gene died nine years ago, and until three years ago, Pat still lived in the house they built for retirement. "Until Gene's death," she says, "I had never lived alone, amazing as that probably seems to a younger generation. At age sixty-three, it was both a challenge and an opportunity to discover myself in a new way. From my current perspective, I know that having the courage to live alone and not jump into another relationship was the best decision I ever made.

"Alone, I discovered who I am as a sovereign individual. I found strengths I didn't know I had. I've explored depths of emotions as never before. And I've studied and traveled and been involved with so many new people. I've learned that alone does not have to mean lonely. And I treasure my solitude."

Pat, who now lives in a townhouse, has traveled to Bali and Greece and Switzerland. A few years ago, she went on a two-and-a-half-month driving tour in the western states, during which she was alone except for two weeks with friends at seminars in Sedona and Taos. When she returned home, she'd put 8,690 miles on the car.

"I now live in a deeply spiritual, culturally rich, and diverse small town. My tastes in art, music, books, and people are eclectic. I'm still involved, doing public relations for organizations, perfecting my speaking skills at Toastmasters, writing a history of my husband's family, plus pursuing my personal studies. I treasure time with friends of all ages, good food, and deep conversation."

This is not to say that life without her closest friend and partner, Gene, has not been difficult, but Pat is able to focus on all the good things. "I think it's important to say that we had never planned out what things we had to do, or places we had to go, in order to avoid regrets later. Even in the last few years—when we knew what was ahead of us but not the timing—we didn't focus on celebrating the 'last' special event or visit with someone.

"At Gene's memorial service, I was truly able to say the only regret I had was not to spend another twenty years with my partner of forty-two years. There were no regrets for things undone, words unsaid, places not visited. We had not put things that were important to us off for a 'someday' that might not come. I would grieve, of course, but not from regret and disappointment.

"Each of us will face the day when we are without someone deeply important to us," Pat continues. "How we are able to move through that time depends a lot on inner preparation and spiritual understanding. Fortunately, I had known since I was ten years old that our essential self isn't what dies, that our spirit lives on. That knowing made facing Gene's death so much easier. And he understood that as well.

"If my experience can assist younger people in looking at choices in a new way, I am grateful."

CHAPTER THREE

Defining a Life of Meaning and Spiritual Growth

S O, Y O U M A Y be asking, how do I go about making retirement choices that I know will contribute to my spiritual and personal growth?

I don't suggest that there's an easy answer or that at
some point you won't abandon one choice for another,
but there is an easy way to begin thinking about it: If you
feel "called" to whatever it is you engage in, then it probably represents an opportunity for meaning and for spiritual growth. If you feel "driven" to it, then chances are
it'll turn out to be another job, a chore, a burdensome
obligation.

The potential conflict in a retirement choice is the
same as the one you faced when starting your career
years ago: which path do you *want* to choose versus
which path do you think you *ought to want* to choose. And

43

society's pressures are very similar to the ones you faced at that time. You'll be encouraged by friends, family, and associates to "get involved," to "do something." You'll hear appeals from organizations to volunteer on their behalf. You'll receive dozens of advertisements and promotions trying to lure you into buying something or joining something. Every travel agent, airline and cruise ship, and vacation home developer will have you on the list. It will require a lot of emotional stamina to resist this stuff, to stay centered and focused, and to reject any influence beyond your own sense of what will help you create a life of meaning.

If you've spent years thinking of yourself as a person who "gets things done," you'll undoubtedly have difficulty letting go of doing, so it will become all the more essential for you to understand that a life of meaning or of personal and spiritual growth is a life of being and not of doing. This is true even in the more active aspects of a spiritual retirement, such as performing community service, renewing family ties, or traveling the world with new eyes. If these very active and relationship-involved pursuits are not embraced in an introspective and reflective way, they can easily become just an extension of your work life, another phase of getting things done, of checking things off the list, of racking up accomplishments, of building that great celestial résumé.

The paradox, of course, is that while you will continue to do something, perhaps very actively, you must approach it from an attitude of being. This is not to suggest that you avoid accomplishments; on the contrary, the basic nature of what you choose may require accomplishment. But the goal of a spiritual life is not in getting done whatever there is to do but in being fully present and conscious in the doing itself. If you've ever heard the expression that life is a journey and not a destination, then now is the time to start really believing it.

> *If you've ever heard the expression that life is a journey and not a destination, then now is the time to start really believing it.*

When as part of my lectures and workshops I talk about expressing one's spiritual values at work or about the confluence of spirituality and work, it is inevitable that I am met with a variety of reactions that, after a decade of dealing with them, have become very predictable. Some people think I'm talking about religion. Others think I'm veering off into New Age mumbo jumbo. I've been told that the subject has no place in a business setting, that spirituality is a personal matter not appropriate for group discussion except, perhaps, at church. I've been met with anger both from religionists who feel that I'm offering a substitute for their beliefs and from nonreligionists who feel that I'm trying to proselytize for some belief system or another.

Frankly, I have tried to avoid defining *spirituality* and instead have concentrated on the personal characteristics that seem to me to evidence people's deeper connections, whether with the great mystery, the ineffable, the higher power, God, or simply their fellow human beings. In the workplace, it is those characteristics and behaviors that define a person, not what that person may feel. Feelings or beliefs must be expressed in behavior, or they can't be made known in any social context, work or otherwise. As I wrote in *The Servant Leader*, "those around you in the workplace . . . can't see inside your head, they can't know what you think or how you feel, they can't subliminally detect your compassion or pain or joy or good will. In other words, the only way you can manifest your . . . spirit in the workplace is through your behavior."

Now, in addressing "spiritual retirement," the challenge to explain and define takes on a different coloration, because in retirement you may not find yourself—or may choose not to be—in a social setting. Or you make seek spiritual expression or spiritual growth not only in relationship with other people but also in singular ways, in more introspective, contemplative, and reflective ways. So while behavior is still the most visible way of expressing your spiritual values with people, your retirement life may lead to a new, or a renewed, focus on your own feelings of spirituality, on your perceptions of what it means to "be spiritual."

Still, this is a difficult subject partly because of some people's feelings of a conflict between "spirituality" and religion and partly because the word *spiritual*, curiously enough, has come so strongly into pop culture that it risks losing any meaning at all beyond a vague feeling about something deeper. Yet as I write this, I'm even reluctant to denigrate the pop culture people who invoke *spirituality* as the word of the moment. After all, who am I to try to invalidate their feelings or question their sincerity?

Given my disinclination toward definition, I believe that the bottom line (as we used to say in business) is this: The discussion, disagreement, confusion, and difficulty of the subject are all essential to the quest for spiritual growth and the search for meaning. The fact that spirituality does not yield to easy definition tells me that the spiritual life is, by its fundamental nature, a life of questioning, exploration, understandings, reexamination, and ever-new understandings. It is a life, as Taoists might describe it, of "not knowing."

Still, it would be presumptuous as well as inaccurate to suggest that the people interviewed for this book would all agree with my observations about the life of spiritual growth. So it is important to sample how some of them think of it or define it.

One former business executive told me that in his view, spirituality is about community as much as anything else—"the feeling of being connected to others," as he put it.

Peter Roy, retired president of Whole Foods, Inc., expands on that point: "It is my spirit that I know is connected to all people, all things. Thus, to me spirituality is the awareness and nurturing of my spirit. My spiritual practice is to consciously 'not forget' about my spirit, my connections to others, all throughout the day and night whether I am picking up the dry cleaning or chopping vegetables."

Kay Riley, who has an M.A. in Spiritual Direction, says, "Simply defined, spirituality is how we connect with God or with the sacred, however we define that. Primarily we connect through our experiences. To me it is relating to all creation with the spirit of openness and love. That perspective gives me a sense of peace and helps me move toward health and wholeness."

Jeanne Cahill, who maintained an active volunteer life while running her successful business, defines an active spirituality: "To me, spiritual acts are those which help define one's thoughts and character as they relate to humanity and nature, a way of living which enhances the soul . . . and which leaves the world a better place because you passed by."

Carol Burns, who says she sees her life as a continuum and doesn't think of her life in phases such as "work life" or "retirement life," claims not to know clearly what she believes as a concept of spirituality but then says, "In my daily life, it's part of my whole person. I try to feel it in whatever I do—conversations with people, the way I talk to my dog, the way I look out the window at nature. I sometimes feel helpless on this subject in the sense that I'm not able to put a handle on exactly how I feel."

Rick Prill, former president of New Hope Natural Media, says that his concept of spirituality has become blended with his own "quote unquote religious beliefs. My view of spirituality is that it's personal religion; I no longer subscribe to a particular religion, but I have a belief in a higher power, in God. I believe that God is best expressed as the collective life force, and my spiritual life involves tapping into that life force whenever possible. I find it in many things that feel nourishing, such as spending time with friends and being of service to others."

John Clark, a vice president of finance, says that his family was always involved in the church, over many generations, but he and his wife, Holly, have become less so. "We are getting our spiritual needs met, but outside the church. We do it by reading books that focus on various aspects of spirituality as well as on the more mysterious aspects of science, such as quantum mechanics."

Holly, who is an adjunct instructor at a local college, sometimes feels rebellious about the church but says she's not trying to influence anyone else about that. "I think you can be spiritual and not religious and religious and not spiritual. But John and I are just as involved in congregational worship, with friends, family, and so on, as if we were in a church. It doesn't have to be a church with a pew."

Mike Kee, former marketing director of an herb sup-plement company, was not brought up in a church but feels he has become strongly spiritual. "I had a little epiphany a few years ago," he says. "I was driving along a highway in New Mexico, and I started thinking about God. I don't have a clear image of God, but a series of things happened: a hawk flew over the car, the sun came up over the mountain, and the clouds seemed to be arranged very beautifully down the valley, and it hit me. This is God. Everything, all this. And I started crying. . . . Now on my daily walk, I stop at a particular rock, sit there, and pray. It has helped through some difficult times."

Throughout these conversations, I found over and over that the essential debate about the word *spiritual* or *spirituality* seems to turn on whether God is involved. But I also found that many of the people called on multiple expressions to describe God, including "higher power," "the great mystery," "the unknown and unknowable," "a higher reality," "the Divine," "the sacred."

The most acceptable and least threatening of the terms seemed to be "the sacred." For religious people, the sacred seemed able to transcend differences between faiths and, within Christianity, differences between de-nominations. For people who are not religious, the sa-cred seemed to describe a sense of something special and perhaps mysterious, something beyond the physical but still not Divine or superhuman.

Thus, the conclusion may be that a spiritual experience is one in which a person feels in the presence of the sacred.

When does this happen, and how does it happen? At many times and in many ways, some that may be surprising. Certainly they need not all feel like epiphanies or sudden brilliant insights or even what might be called religious experiences. It's easy to imagine that you are in the presence of the sacred when you're standing among the great redwoods of the West or when you're at a particularly moving dramatic performance or at the birth of a baby, but it can be just as easy when you're having an evening with friends or at a family reunion or driving on a country road. The key is how you perceive, and feel about, these experiences: What emotional response, what mood, do they evoke? In fact, the goal of a spiritual life is to feel in the presence of the sacred at all times, wherever you are and whatever you're doing.

But this is not a decision or an event or an episode; it is a thoughtful, deliberate, and often contemplative process involving preparation, discipline, and positive intent. The Reverend James Newby, author of *Sacred Chaos*, pointed out in a sermon several weeks after the terrorist attacks of September 11, 2001, that sometimes spiritual experiences "burst upon us from the outside, as in the death of a friend or loved one." Rick Prill agrees. "When my father died, my sister, who claimed to have no spiritual feelings whatsoever, said to me, 'How can I not believe he's going to be with other beautiful souls?' Dad's death awakened her feelings of spirituality, and she has been spiritual ever since."

But Reverend Newby also describes a process that requires "staying awake spiritually by practicing the art of compassion in all of the great and small acts of caring that we do for one another."

Then he suggests that we cleanse ourselves physically so that we are more awakened spiritually. He doesn't mean to practice some arcane bathing or purging ritual or take special herbs and supplements. He is referring to all the things in today's world that get in the way of spirituality, "from television to telephones." To identify your own "spiritual obstructions," he suggests asking yourself, "What are those things . . . that get in the way of my ability to stay awake spiritually?"

Finally, Reverend Newby says, "We can stay awake spiritually by tempering our self-righteousness and seeking to live in a spirit of humility."

So, practice the art of compassion, cleanse yourself of a lot of the pointless stuff in your life, and let go of ego and self-righteousness. Not easy, but if you're successful, you can achieve those personal characteristics that I believe will assure you of a life in which you feel that everything you do has a spiritual component and in which you feel always in the presence of the sacred.

Those characteristics of the spiritual life include:

Gratitude and reverence. The Christian mystic Meister Eckhardt wrote, "In praying it is enough to say 'thank you.'" This means living in gratitude that you are alive, that you have family and friends, that with all its troubles the Earth is still a beautiful place and you are free to enjoy it. It means saying or thinking the words *thank you* every time you recognize that you are experiencing something for which you are grateful. It also means adopting an attitude of plenty rather than of scarcity. On the bulletin board of my office is a sign with a message worth repeating to yourself every day: "What you have is enough."

> *It means saying or thinking the words* thank you *every time you recognize that you are experiencing something for which you are grateful.*

And people who live in gratitude live also in awareness of the great mystery and often feel the presence of the sacred.

This attitude need not be as ethereal as it sounds. A middle-aged single father told me, "When I got full custody of my thirteen-year-old daughter, it was as if I came face-to-face with a higher calling. It changed everything about my perceptions of who I was, and I swear to you, Jim, when I'm helping her with homework or watching her at a dance lesson, I feel I'm on another plane. It's almost like an altered state. Sometimes I'm overcome with the sheer happiness of how my life has changed, and I know it's changed forever. Does that sound crazy?"

It didn't. What it sounded like was awe, like reverence for a life beyond doing, beyond our traditional definitions of success. It was the sound of someone who felt the sacred in the very everydayness of fatherhood.

Living in an attitude of gratitude and reverence opens the possibilities for making spirituality real in almost anything you choose to engage.

Presence and a sense of beginning. The Buddhists call this "nowness." It has always struck me as profoundly mysterious that everything that has ever happened since the beginning of time comes down to this very instant, and this one, and this one. Which, I think, tells us only one thing: Make the most of these instants because these are the only instants we're living—not yesterday's, not tomorrow's. To paraphrase another Buddhist saying, if you are angry, you're living in the past; if you're fearful or anxious, you're living in the future. Learn from the past and plan for the future—but live in the present.

As you get older, as you approach retirement, and after you retire, the art of living in the present, of living each day for all it has to offer—as the twelve-steppers say, "one day at a time"—becomes ever more important. Two destructive maladies unfortunately are revealed far too often among people who have retired: looking back and living all the past glories over and over again, and looking forward with an existential dread of the big deadline.

The cure, as well as the preventive, for those maladies is simply focusing your attention and energies on now and working to imbue every single day with opportunity for meaning and growth. Some people refer to this as always having a "sense of beginning," a feeling that everything in life begins again every day. You've heard the cliché about today being the first day of the rest of your life? Well, like a lot of clichés, it's based on truth.

I heard it put another way one time. In my youth in the South, I liked to hunt quail. I liked the ritual of it, the relationship with the dogs, the outdoors—all of it, including eating the quail. I often hunted with an older man who would lead me over hills and into bottoms and through heavy weeds, all the while giving me a running commentary on how things used to be. "There used to be a covey on that fence row over there," he'd say, pointing to the row of scrub trees. Then pointing in another direction, he'd say, "And I used to get a lot of birds along that little creek, between the bean field and the ditch." He'd go on and on with these hunting stories of how things used to be, and I got so used to it that I considered it part of the hunting ritual.

But one day he stopped in midsentence, looked at me, and said, "You know something, Jimmy, you can't eat them damned used-to-be birds." It was as good a piece of philosophy as anyone ever shared with me about staying focused on the present.

A capacity for discovery and surprise. As we age, there is the great temptation to feel that we now know a thing or two about life and that there is little left to learn. But people who are successful in living a life of meaning, either before or after retirement, realize that learning is almost synonymous with growing.

A very successful and respected executive in the publishing business retired a few years ago. Immediately he was approached by other large companies in that same industry, asking him to serve on their boards of directors. He turned them all down. When I asked him why, he said, "This may sound arrogant, but I truly don't believe there was much more I could learn in that business. Certainly there wasn't much more I wanted to learn, so I decided that if I was going to serve on any boards, for-profit or nonprofit, the one criterion would be that I'd have the opportunity to learn something."

Colonel Tom Sawner said that when he was readying himself for retirement, he knew he wanted to use his skills and talents in training leaders, but he also knew he wanted to keep learning new things. He remained open to all possibilities, and still does, because his quest, he said, is to reach out and find what will create meaning in his life.

Spencer Longshore III, a highly successful advertising executive, now fifty-four years old, says, "I don't know all the things I'll do at retirement, but I know they won't be what I have been doing. I want to learn other things, contribute in other ways. I don't have a clue what that will be, but it'll be something I can learn and grow from. And I know this: I'm not being analytical about it, the way I've always been, writing things down on a legal pad, seeing how all the pieces fit together. It'll have to be a calling when it comes. I'm remaining open, trying to keep my whole consciousness clear. 'Surprise me, God.'"

Generosity and a passion for service. Probably nothing is more fundamentally spiritual than an attitude of generosity, which then evokes an inclination to always be open to ways that you can serve others. If you live in gratitude, believing that what you have is enough, then you likely will be inclined to want to share whatever it is—time, talents, financial resources—with others.

But this is not about the traditional approach to charity. "Giving money is the easy part," one about-to-be-retired engineer told me. "The hard part is to give of yourself, to take time and make the effort to seek out people who really need what you have to offer."

Even harder is for you to feel gratitude that you've been given the opportunity to serve, rather than expecting gratitude from those you serve.

I was greatly moved in a conversation with retired editor-photographer David Jordan when he told me that early in his retirement he would volunteer time at the hospital to hold the "preemies," the babies who'd been born prematurely and who needed human contact as part of their development. Imagine that—this big man sitting calmly, holding and talking to these tiniest of humans.

The paradox about people of generous spirits and a passion for service is that, in their acts of generosity, they feel that they are the ones receiving the benefit, that they are the ones being served. And, in turn, they are grateful.

AT THIS POINT, you no doubt have surmised that spirituality, the spiritual life, and/or the life of meaning do not yield to definitions that satisfy everyone. Fortunately, they don't have to. This is about your journey and no one else's. You are the only one who can decide how words like *spiritual* and *meaning* and *personal growth* fit into your notions of what your life is and how you want it to be. Sam Keen, in his astonishing book *Hymns to an Unknown God*, writes, "The search for spirit, for God, is ultimately the quest to know ourselves in our heights and depths. . . . It was, is, and always will be the greatest human adventure."

So the quest for a life of meaning and spiritual growth begins inside you, but I admit that this journey is easier to describe than to do. One woman who regards herself as "very spiritual" puts it this way: "It's like some people talk about art. I know it when I feel it."

If her approach works for you, too, it's good enough.

KEN AND PEG'S STORY

Sometimes You Don't Even Notice Retirement

The friends of Ken and Peg McDougall hardly noticed when they retired. In fact, Ken and Peg hardly noticed it. While they did some financial planning, they never gave a thought to planning for a life of meaning and spiritual growth. They were already living it.

"Continuing to grow spiritually is just part of who we are," says Ken. "Our motivation has always been to follow the commandment 'Love thy neighbor as thyself.' We haven't made a conscious effort to change after we retired, and we haven't made a conscious effort to continue. We just went on with what we were doing."

Involvement in the church—Christian Church (Disciples of Christ)—has been the foundation of Ken and Peg's life together since they were first married. Ken had been raised in the Methodist Church and Peg in the Christian Church (Disciples of Christ); after a few years of marriage they both became charter members of a Christian Church in their community.

"Because of our Christian faith and our connection with the church, we've remained alert to opportunities to serve," Peg says.

The list of their activities in the service of others is almost overwhelming in size and scope. Some years ago, they sponsored a Laotian family, and they've been part of that family's life ever since. In 2001, they cochaired a committee that sponsored three Sudanese "lost boys," who now, according to Ken, "dominate our lives. It's much like raising teenagers all over again."

Between them, Ken and Peg have served in almost every office of their church. Peg, who was named a YWCA Woman of Achievement, founded a church prekindergarten program and later served as director of a day care center at a Methodist church. She continues to volunteer at a social service agency that serves people who are homeless or living in poverty, operates a day care center, helps people with parenting skills in a Parents Anonymous program, and provides a special Christmas Sharing Program, among other services.

Ken has worked as development director of an area religious council, and he serves or has served on boards of a retirement home, a pastoral counseling center, a children's cancer program, and others. He is currently a member of the board of his church.

In 1964, inspired by his pastor, Ken went to Mississippi for the famous "Mississippi Summer," during which civil rights volunteers, most of them white north-erners, registered African Americans to vote. "That may have been my first really personal service. It was only a week's experience, but it was life changing in that it made me acutely aware of the needs people have in this world in which we live." Was it dangerous? "Yes," Ken admits, "but also fascinating."

Ken and Peg have served in many situations together. Perhaps the most spiritually uplifting, as well as challenging, experience came when Peg became the volunteer resident manager of a Ronald McDonald House, serving the families of seriously ill children. She and Ken moved in for two years where they acted, in Ken's words, as "compassionate innkeepers."

"The most demanding thing was just being there for people," he explains. "You had to be there in all circumstances. The people would look to us for comfort, for someone to just talk to. The worst experience of all was when a child died while the parents were at the house." Ken is still saddened at the memory. "In the health care field, you're taught to remain aloof," he says, "but it was just impossible. The only good outcome is that we still hear, years later, from some of those parents just because they wanted to stay in touch with someone who'd been with them at that difficult time."

After they told me about volunteering with the National Park Service's Golden Gate National Recreation Area in California, a six-week experience, I asked whether they ever did anything just for fun. They admit that, in retirement, they decided against a life of travel and recreation in favor of continuing their service to others, yet they love attending the symphony and good films, as well as doing crafts.

"You'd think that, at age seventy-seven, I'd be ready to sit back and let other people do some of these things,"

Ken says, "but the needs are great, and we believe that being spiritual is to try every day to follow Jesus' commandment about loving our neighbors. We fall short, of course, but we try."

PART TWO

Time for Those You Love

WE GET OUT of touch. There's no other way to put it. In the demands of our work lives and in our incessant attempts to respond in a way that assures our professional success, we simply get out of touch with the people who mean the most to us. We have a reservoir of excuses, but they all boil down to the pressures of time.

Family and friends who for years were part of our very lives simply fade from our consciousness except perhaps during the holidays when we may send a card or, sad to say, when there's a death and we gather for the funeral.

It's not that we don't want to see them—sometimes we even intend to see them—but it becomes a matter of priorities. Do we abandon or diminish our professional social contacts to make room for far-flung friends? Do we give up precious time with the kids in order to see other family members? After all, how much effort should we put into maintaining connections that have become weaker with time and that often depend more on nostalgia than on shared present-day interests and experiences?

All of us have to answer these questions for ourselves, but as retirement approaches and as we age, our professional contacts—the people we are connected to only by mutual association and interest and not by affection and shared life stories—begin to fade in importance. (This is not to say that some of your colleagues, coworkers, and professional contacts don't also develop into close and intimate friends over the years, but in those cases, the connections have transcended the workplace and no longer exist just because of your work life. These relationships will often continue to be part of your life beyond work.)

In your planning for a retirement life of meaning and purpose, the need to answer author Sam Keen's questions "Where am I going, and who is going with me?" takes on increasing urgency. And the answers are more likely to involve the people who have helped you become who you are rather than the people who were part of what you did.

Unfortunately, the friendships and family connections you wish to renew will not fade back into your life as they faded away. Renewing them will require effort and intention.

We need not examine the world of dysfunctional relationships to realize that the path of love is perilous, often filled with the obstacles of old misunderstandings and grievances. Thus, the first step toward renewing connections important to you is to review honestly those relationships and identify any need for forgiveness and reconciliation. Then be brave. Take the first step. Be the first to seek forgiveness. Demonstrate that you value the relationship more than you value your own ego. You will be amazed how this act of humility will clear the way for reconciliation.

> *Be the first to seek forgiveness. Demonstrate that you value the relationship more than you value your own ego.*

There are many ways to go about the process of renewing the connections with those you love and who love you, and no one way works for everyone, thus I hope the anecdotes and stories in this section help you determine how to reembrace the people who can once again become so important throughout the rest of your life.

RICK'S STORY
Retiring Before Retirement

Many people don't wait until "official" retirement before they retire. The fortunate ones make the decision as a result of advantageous finances or a desire to try something else or the simple attraction of a new life. Rick Prill had a different reason for his decision: He went through a life-changing experience that made him realize what he most wanted to do was help other people in his same situation.

Perhaps the story of Rick's retirement began when he realized his chances were slim. In effect, the doctors had almost pronounced a death sentence, and now he found himself in a southern evangelical church surrounded by fervent worshippers who were giving him a "laying on of hands."

What am I doing here, he thought. I don't know any of these people, and if my cousin hadn't hooked me up with them, I would never have volunteered to do something like this.

Then, he later told me, "Whether it had anything to do with the success of the surgery and the tumor going away, I don't know, but I certainly did feel the love force of those people."

Several months before the laying on of hands, Rick had been diagnosed with a tumor that was, for lack of a better description, so entwined with his lower spine that the doctors felt it was inoperable. After a nationwide search, Rick found a surgeon who had done similar operations and was willing to make the attempt with Rick. There was very little expectation of success. Even if the tumor was removed, paralysis or other unpredictable results were probable.

When the decision to do the surgery was made, Rick had three days to get his life in order. "I had to get ready to die," he says. "I had to resolve things emotionally with other people with only three days to do it. Then I thought, this is the way it is for everyone. We only have the rest of our lives to get ready; it's just that the rest of my life is likely only going to be three more days."

Rick was facing bankruptcy at the time, so he knew there was nothing he could do financially in three days, but, he says, "The situation demanded that I have some spiritual resolution with people in my life. During those three days, I called people, sought reconciliation and forgiveness, and vice versa. But mostly these calls just turned out to be expressions of love."

Looking back on that experience, he says, "The process was really powerful, and it changed my life forever. You know, we're all facing death, maybe in twenty years rather than three days, but we all have to do the same things: reestablish loving relationships, seek forgiveness and reconciliation, and affirm the importance of those relationships to one another."

After the successful surgery, Rick determined that he would turn this experience into something positive for other people. It was like an awakening to a connection with everyone else in the world. "I don't really feel the laying on of hands had anything to do with making the tumor go away, but I respected and appreciated those people. I don't subscribe to a particular religion, but I do believe in a higher power, in God, but mostly as a collective life force. The process of my own spirituality is tapping into that force whenever possible.

"I do it by spending time with friends. And service to others feels even more spiritually nourishing."

After the surgery, Rick went to his ranch in Colorado. "It was really just a shack," he says, "but lying there I was thinking that if I was able to walk, if I was able to function, I'd figure out a way to put some energy back into others, perhaps by providing a place like a spiritual retreat for those who had a terminal illness or otherwise were coming to grips with death."

Rick lay in his bed in that little shack, and, as in the stories of prisoners of war who have designed their dream houses in their heads, he designed his spiritual retreat.

His life partner, Mike Kee, former marketing director of an herb supplement company, says, "We picture this as a place where someone who has been diagnosed with a terminal illness can come. They can read books, watch videos, be with us, get counseling." Then he adds, "Or they can just be irrationally angry. They should be allowed to be angry, to walk the land and scream at the mountains if they want to."

Rick adds an explanatory note: "When I was told it was all over, I felt screwed. I was angry. I started driving recklessly one day and almost killed Mike and me. I realized then that people have to have a way and a place to process the anger or just blow it off."

After the surgery, Rick went back to work and within a few years became president of a media company in the natural products field. He managed to overcome his financial problems, and now, working part-time, he and Mike have spent these past years working on their dream. They've expanded their house, renovated an old guest house, and built a six-thousand-square-foot building with bedrooms and bathrooms to accommodate as many as fifty people for larger gatherings.

"We need to have it be enough of a business that we can pay the bills," Rick explains, "but not make a lot of money. We're hoping to align ourselves with a hospice program or medical facility, and we have a close friend who is a bereavement counselor. She's very excited about the prospects."

Rick and Mike agree that they're taking a big risk with the money they've put aside for retirement. "But there comes a time," Rick says, "when you have to ask the question 'How much money is enough?' At a certain point you have to make a decision that, from a real security standpoint, there will never be enough money. So we just decided to try for some kind of sustainable cash flow and still have our place fulfill our vision of serving others."

Both Rick and Mike also are determined to spend more time with the people they love—parents, siblings, and friends. "I don't want to look back ten years from now," says Rick, "and say, 'I wanted so much to spend time with so-and-so who is now dead.'

"One thing you learn on your deathbed, which is where I literally thought I was, is that this life is about loving and serving others and taking time to do it."

CHAPTER FOUR

Appreciating Your Roots

You are
in these hills
who you were and who you will become
and not just who you are. . . .

—"Genealogy," from *Nights Under a Tin Roof*

I'M A SOUTHERNER by birth and have lived in the North for forty-two years. One of the little social differences I've noticed between the South and almost anywhere else is that when two southerners meet their first question is "Where are you from?" The next question is "Who are your people?" Only after establishing place and people might they ask, "What do you do?" So it was an adjustment, if not a shock, traveling to the East and

West Coasts and throughout the Midwest on business, to find that everywhere else, it's the "do" question that comes first.

In retirement, it's the "do" question that disappears. No one will ask what you do anymore, though there may be those people stuck in the past who will want to know what you did so they can talk about what they did. There's nothing particularly wrong with looking back from time to time and thinking about the old career and the old accomplishments, just for the sake of a little nostalgia, if nothing else. But a more productive examination of the past is one through which you focus on who you are and on who are, and were, your people.

Honoring the Ancestors

Genealogy can become an engaging and fulfilling journey, but you need not go at it full-time to learn about your forebears. "Why do it at all?" you might ask. Jeanne Cahill answers this way: "One thing I have tried to do is give my children a sense of who they are in a long line of ancestors and also a love of the land where our ancestors trod."

Jeanne began work on a genealogy forty-five years ago, as a young mother. She turned her notes over to a distant cousin who was committed enough to the project that she produced a book entitled *The Ten Taylor Children*. Jeanne's great-grandfather was one of the ten.

"I bought the book for each of my children," she continues, "so they have a written record of their ancestors on at least one branch of the tree."

Jeanne and her family feel rooted to the "long-leaf pine/wiregrass area of Georgia" where her ancestors lived from the late 1700s. "My children are all aware of the need to leave this Earth in better condition than we found it, a lesson my father instilled in me and I have instilled in my children. Daddy called it our stewardship of what we have in the land." (See more of Jeanne's story, page 208.)

DO I EXPLORE my own roots? In many ways. About twenty-six years ago, my mother died. Then about twenty years ago my father died; six months later my brother died. This left me the oldest living man in the family, and I was only forty-nine at the time. Suddenly, it seemed, there was no one left in the world who still thought of me as a boy, which meant it was truly the end of childhood.

It also meant that my grandchildren, living in Iowa and never having even visited the South, would not be connected with either that place or those people unless I made some effort to teach them the old stories. I try to do that, less successfully than I'd like, and I hope my poetry and other writings will give them a way to connect with what they must think of as an ancient world. My first book of poetry, *Nights Under a Tin Roof*, is an intentional effort to keep alive the recollections of a southern boyhood.

I was asked to write a poem commemorating the 150th anniversary of the little church in Mississippi that was pastored by both my grandfather and my father. The poem is engraved on a monument in the church cemetery and surely will be there long after I'm gone.

I visit family, of course, and because I live "up north" now, my Mississippi family usually rolls out some kind of prodigal son feast when I return: all the good old dishes from fried chicken and barbecue to banana pudding and caramel cake. The food itself takes us all back to an earlier time when food came less easily but when the fellowship of Sunday dinner was for many families the most important event of the week.

At least once every summer I barbecue a couple of pork shoulders for my family in Iowa. It becomes a "roots" event, at which I put on tapes of old-time gospel music and even dress in bib overalls to do the cooking. I am very blessed to have sons and a daughter-in-law and grandchildren and a wife who indulge this high-fat exercise in nostalgia. And I confess that I hope someone in the group is watching to see how it's done.

I'm equally blessed to be part of my wife's family, which is the most loving group of people I've ever witnessed at close hand. There are five siblings and nine grandchildren, and everyone in the family puts a high priority on getting together at holidays. Some of the older grandchildren are scattered now, but most work hard at getting "home" at least for Christmas.

When I was younger, I had a very low tolerance for noise and chaos in the house, but retirement (or maybe just aging) has made me deeply grateful for these gatherings, which always remind me of a line toward the end of John Irving's novel *The Water Method Man*, in which he looks around the room and feels gratitude for all "this beloved flesh."

And I know that someday the things the family does together will become part of the roots experience of our young people and children who, it must be admitted, are now sometimes only marginally tolerant of these gatherings.

A RETIRED SCHOOL superintendent told me that in the schools he supervised, he had seen so many young people who seemed rootless and unconnected that he became committed to assuring that the young people of his family had at least some exposure to other members of the family, no matter how distant, as well as to their own piece of history. He became the driving force behind a three-family reunion that gathers every other year.

In addition, he encouraged and contributed to a family history, plus collected contributions from family members to place a headstone at the grave of his great-great-grandfather deep in what is now a national forest.

"I want children to be able to go there years from now," he says, "and see the grave of the man responsible for starting this branch of the family. He was a man who braved all kinds of dangers to make the trip, then to clear the land and establish his homestead. That's important for kids to try to understand because it's so far removed from their own experience."

He adds, "It's kinda like in the Far East, I guess, in that I want all of us to honor our ancestors."

Death and Dying

Alphonse de Lamartine said, "Sometimes when one person is missing, the whole world seems depopulated." How true that is, particularly when that person has been one of the emotional anchors of your life.

The passing of a loved one, with all its tragedy, can also offer an opportunity for service as well as for reconnection.

There is no good news on this subject, but there is comfort. The rituals surrounding dire illness and death often serve to reconnect us deeply with those who are dying and with those who share our grief. To repeat the observation of Reverend Jim Newby, "Sometimes spiritual experiences are thrust upon us unexpectedly."

The passing of a loved one, with all its tragedy, can also offer an opportunity for service as well as for reconnection. At those times, all the barriers of ego are down,

all the self-consciousness disappears, all the little dis-
agreements melt away.

Margie Daly, a successful magazine editor and writer
now retired, tells of a last episode with her mother:

> I found my love for her easy and tender—probably safer,
> too, compared to earlier times with the difficult
> mother–daughter dance. A seminal anecdote: As she be-
> came more childlike . . . she reverted to eating just with a
> spoon and her fingers. I managed to take her out to lunch
> almost until the end. . . . Conversations were endlessly
> repetitive. She was especially happy to be out and eating
> her favorite food, spaghetti and red sauce. I learned to
> order stacks of paper napkins and simply wipe off her
> hands again and again. She'd accept the fork with a smile,
> then revert to spoon and fingers once more, then scratch
> her head or straighten her glasses. . . . [S]he had beautiful
> white hair so you can imagine the colorful display. . . .
> I've never had a toddler, so I was new at this, but I found it
> tremendously endearing.

WHEN HIS FATHER died, Peter Roy, realizing that
many of his baby-boomer friends would soon be losing
their parents, decided to share his experience with them.
In an eloquent e-mail, he wrote:

> Dear Friends,
>
> To bring some closure to this whole process I wanted to
> share with you what the last 72 hours of my Dad's life was

like and what I learned from it. So many of us are at the age where we will be soon faced with the death of a parent and perhaps the experience my family went through this week can help you when you are faced with similar circumstances. . . .

He only lived 72 hours after the stroke, but that was enough time for his whole family to get back to New Orleans to be with him in his final hours and to be of total service to him. . . . The best decision we made all week was to pull him out of the hospital and take him home to die.

Being at home was so much better for him and his family and enabled us to create such a supportive environment for his passing . . . [and] his consciousness was with us until the very end. There was no doubt in any of our minds that he could hear what we were saying. He would often respond to what was being said in any small way he could. We were laughing and carrying on, telling funny stories about him and our childhoods and he would open an eye or wiggle a finger to add his two cents. . . .

At the moment of his death, I was holding his head in my hands and all of his children and four of five of his grandchildren had their hands on his body telling him we loved him and it was OK to go. May we all be so blessed to die in such a supportive environment!

The funeral was on Monday and it was quite an event. Right before the public visitation, our family and a few friends gathered around his casket to pay our last respects and to give him anything he may need to "take along for the ride." It was very funny. Perhaps my Dad's favorite thing to do was to go out to dinner with friends and he always would pick up the check. So I slipped his Visa card in his pocket and his grandfather's gold pen so he would be prepared wherever he was going next to get the check. His grandsons put menus in from his favorite restaurants; . . . [friends] put in a ceramic frog, which is a symbol of safe journey. My sisters offered up sentimental symbols of their relationship with him. It was great. Before we let the public in, I retied his tie for him. . . . [H]e never wore a slip knot in his life; he was definitely a Windsor knot man.

The cast of characters that showed up to pay their last respects was not to be believed. Former schoolmates, patients, friends, employees, waiters, store clerks, bookies, people young and old all showed up. As I stood in the receiving line, I heard story after story about how my Dad's greatest strength as a human being was his ability to make all people feel special and to feel good about themselves. What a gift and what a lesson!

When it came my turn to eulogize him, I tried my best to share what it was like to be Billy Roy's son. Everyone else knew him as a friend, doctor, employer, golfing buddy, or customer, but no one else knew him as a son knows his father. It was the toughest public speaking gig I have ever had to do. I tried my best to hold it together enough to share that he was a man that cared so much about some things and so very little about others. He was always there for his children, patients, and friends, but he could not have cared less about the cars he drove (Volkswagen bugs), the clothes he wore, or the clubs he belonged to. . . . I also shared something that I have realized over the last few years as I have gotten to know myself better, and that is that the traits people love and appreciate in me are the same traits I share with my father.

The night of his funeral, I rented a private room at Antoine's, one of his favorite restaurants, and we had twenty-six people to dinner to share stories and celebrate his life. We kept an empty chair for him and there was no doubt he was there in spirit and had a great time. We told stories and laughed until we cried. It was a wonderful party, and I signed the check to his account. I know this was one check he would have insisted on paying.

The entire process of his dying has been one of the most profound and healing experiences of my life and the same is true for my sisters and our entire family. His last gift to us was so meaningful. He pulled us all together and through me and my sisters led our family through such an amazing process. A final gift in a life worth living.

IN CONVERSATION AFTER conversation, I heard frequent references to death and the coming reality of it. "I realize I have less time to live than I've already lived," one man told me. A fifty-year-old said, "My friends all kid themselves by having 'half-time' parties, but we all know that three-quarters of our lives are over."

Mark Haverland, who is a member of a support group of people of similar ages and circumstances, says, "Like it or not, we have to admit the anxiety about death."

"The only good thing about facing our own mortality," said another man, "is that it focuses your attention."

Exactly. It is at this time of life that we naturally begin to focus on what's important. Rick Prill had a more dramatic experience than most of us. Diagnosed a few years ago with an inoperable tumor, "I had to get myself together," he says, "had to resolve things emotionally with other people, had to get ready to die . . . and I only had three days to do it." (See his full story, page 68.)

A Commitment to Staying Connected

Fortunately we don't have to wait for death or a health crisis to nurture the connections with our families.

If genealogy is appealing, there are myriad ways to go about it: clubs, Web sites, software, and (still) libraries. And don't forget those treasure troves of information: the county courthouses with their old records. Norman Van Klompenburg (see his story, page 90) has used all these resources in tracing his family, who settled from the Netherlands, and his wife's family, which has connections back to the *Mayflower*. The Van Klompenburgs' children and grandchildren are all involved together in this exploration of their roots.

TRACING YOUR FAMILY'S ROOTS

Before you start a genealogy search, give some thought to these questions and exercises. Similar to the "thinking/doing" questions in chapter 2, they will help you focus your search so you have a more satisfying journey and outcome.

1. What is your purpose in wanting to trace your family's roots? Your search will be different depending on whether you're looking for names, colorful events, or a deeper connection with your history or with relatives.

2. Spend some time going over whatever old family photos you have. Try to do this in a reflective or meditative frame of mind, and focus on the feelings that come up for you about your family.

3. Make a list of questions you've always wondered about your family and its members.

4. List the things you already know about your family's history that have stuck with you over the years. These might be helpful in guiding your search.

5. Who in your family might like to join you in this search? What strengths and resources can others bring to help in the search? Make a plan for sharing jobs and areas of inquiry.

Some General Sources to Get You Started

The Internet is the best place to do genealogy research because of its capabilities for storing and accessing records and databases. One of the best search engines is www.google.com. Just type in keywords about genealogy, tracing roots, even names, and start checking out sites.

www.Ancestry.com is a megasite that runs www.genealogy.org, billed as the oldest and largest free site, and RootsWeb.com, a how-to site with databases, message boards, and other resources. Ancestry.com is a subscription service (with some free services) offering access to U.S. Census records (they just added 1930 records), Census images, a U.K./Ireland collection, and access to a historical newspapers collection.

www.genhomepage.com lists other genealogy sites for free and offers shareware tools and files. It has a search engine for surnames listed on sites and links to guides, libraries, records, and more.

www.genealogytoolbox.com helps you learn how to use tools for searching. Categories include computers, media, people, places, supplies and services, original records, how-to, and help.

(continues)

85

www.genealogy.about.com also has lots of search tips, plus it lists magazines and books, software, and other product descriptions and top picks. This site is run by Kimberly Powell, professional genealogist, author, Internet consultant, and Web developer.

www.cyndislist.com is a periodically updated listing of Web sites about genealogy; it currently has more than 131,000 links. It features an alphabetical index, topical index, and main index with a search function. This site offers you a good overview of what information is out there about tracing your roots. It's also hosted by RootsWeb.

Clubs, Societies, and Organizations

www.genealogyforum.rootsweb.com/gfaol/internet/Clubs.htm offers a large listing that includes links to the National Genealogy Society, international groups, and more specialized groups.

Roy Reese (see his story, page 164) serves as the informal family historian and keeps the family history on his computer, which gives him a way to stay in current contact with the extended family. He has records of the earliest entries from Europe as well as the latest births of descendants.

If you want to organize a family reunion, there are just as many resources for that as well, plus plenty of accommo-

BEFORE PLANNING THE REUNION

As you're thinking about having a reunion, give some thought to these questions and exercises. They'll help you sort out your reasons for getting together.

1. Think about why you want to have a family gathering. What do you hope it accomplishes? What's motivating you to have a reunion?

2. Look through your family photos, holiday cards, and other correspondence you might have collected over the years. Try to feel the spirit of your family.

3. Think about the intangible gifts each member would bring to such a gathering and ways you could best celebrate their gifts. Make these unique to your family.

4. Before you have the first reunion, list ways you can keep the reunions going. Share these with the other members at the reunion.

dations who'll help put it together. The research and the logistics are not the hard part. The hard part is the commitment, the willingness to be responsible for the outcome you desire, and the loving intention to overcome those things besides geography that have kept your family apart.

Perhaps genealogy and family reunions are not what you need or not what your family will respond to. If

HELPFUL RESOURCES FOR
FAMILY REUNION PLANNING

Reunion Center on www.genealogyforum.roots web.com is a compendium of resources for family reunions. You will find information on planning the reunion, finding relatives, even publishing your own family history and/or newsletter. Many families are organizing into family associations for the purpose of having reunions and sharing genealogical information. The site has a directory of these family associations and of family newsletters. You can also post your family announcements online and get on the site's online reunion schedule.

http://family-reunion.com is a cheerful site with Mister Spiffy, the family reunion doctor trained in helping families with all aspects of planning and sustaining reunions.

Reunions Magazine, PO Box 11727, Milwaukee, WI 53211-0727, provides resources for planning reunions and keeping them alive, along with a workbook for planning. Six issues cost $18; the workbook is $10. The Web site is at www.reunionsmag.com.

The Family Reunion Sourcebook, by Edith Wagner (Lowell House, 1999).

that's the case, the simple everyday things can still help people stay in touch. They're called letters (yes, including e-mails) and phone calls.

Several members of Roy Reese's family keep a continuous "round robin" letter going at all times. Each participant, upon receiving the letter, writes a new one and sends it on. "This means a letter about four to six times a year," Roy explains. "It lets you know you still have blood kin interested in your well-being. This has been going on so long in my family nobody can remember when it began."

My eighty-six-year-old stepmother is an avid computer user. She is a writer and photographer, still actively pursuing both those interests, and she has embraced technology with enthusiasm. A few years ago, I asked my sister what our mother would like for Christmas. "She needs a scanner," came the reply. I couldn't help thinking, "Not a lace doily or a sweater or another little what-not for the house, but a scanner!" So our family stays very much in touch by sending e-mail and photographs regularly over the Internet. That's not unusual, of course; what's important is that it is deliberate and intentional on our parts to use the technology to overcome the geographic distances between us.

Even such simple ideas as these can keep you connected and can help give meaning to your retirement life.

NORMAN'S STORY
Taking the Best of the Job with You

"We didn't go on tour; we just went to work." That was Norman Van Klompenburg's response when asked what he and his wife did after his retirement.

"I don't think my life is much different in retirement than before. As executive director of a community mental health and substance abuse center, a nonprofit, I really feel I was doing something that meets the criteria of a 'life of meaning.' I still see myself as an advocate, somebody who can contribute to change. Only now I'm doing it for free and at my own pace."

Norm admits that there are parts of the job he no longer does or misses. "The administrative or management part I left behind. I don't have to make sure the funding is coming or watch the budget or make sure the people are being effective and doing what needs to be done. But the fulfilling program and service work I can still do. That's a major positive change for me."

He suspects that his life will change somewhat the further he gets into retirement. "I'm doing stuff now as a result of some of the connections I've had professionally. As the years go on, I think I can still be of value to somebody but could pursue it in other ways. Part of my ambition is to join with a group of other retired professionals in some kind of global service activity."

Norm emphasizes that in planning his retirement, a major issue was financial security because the majority of his career was spent in nonprofit organizations that are not known for good retirement packages. "I know this isn't the subject of your book," he says, "but reasonable financial security is necessary to allow for many of the activities we wanted to do. Fortunately, we set up a savings program along with retirement set-asides. With Social Security we think we made adequate preparations."

He also expects his interests to broaden in time and plans to reembrace a broad range of hobby interests he developed over the years including woodworking, metalworking, fishing, boating, and classic cars.

"My plans have always included spending more time pursuing some of these interests, and I hope to find the time in retirement to do that."

Considering the broad range of activities and interests in Norm's life, however, time may indeed be the challenge. His wife, Pat, children, and grandchildren have become involved in the genealogy of their families. There is a *Mayflower* connection, John Alden. Another part of the family has connections to Daniel Boone.

Using the Web to verify their findings, they have located graves of ancestors, discovered records in old courthouse files, and have been able to find stories and documents connecting their families to interesting events in history. Norm and Pat plan to assemble all this material for their grandchildren.

They also plan to spend more time in South Dakota, where they lived for a while, visiting the old neighborhood and seeing old friends. And they'll go back to visit an older brother in the place where Norman grew up. "My brother enjoys showing sheep," Norm says, "so it's kind of fun for me to help him on the farm. Before retirement, I didn't do as much of this kind of activity."

Within all those intentions and interests, however, it is Norm's devotion to helping others that still occupies most of his time. His professional training was in clinical social work and human services administration. "That work has always been challenging and fulfilling for me," he says, "so most of my volunteer work has revolved around this area as well."

When asked about his concept of spirituality, Norm responds that it is to him "a particularly broad thing. It used to represent a particular set of religious beliefs, but that's changed. It now refers to the fulfillment of some deeper meaning." He has been very active in the United Church of Christ, serving on boards and committees, including the church's national commission on racial justice.

"That was kind of an interesting experience for a midwestern boy to get exposed to," Norm says. "It led to my finally becoming chair of the executive council. Then I went back to my local church."

Still today he maintains active involvement in the church as well as a variety of professional and service organizations. "This keeps me in touch with professionals and issues relating to people in need. I also have the opportunity to serve with some groups that continue to advocate for public policy changes that will benefit needy people."

While Norm has succeeded admirably within the structure and organization of the church, his original motivation in getting involved was not about councils and committees, nor was it particularly about personal worship experiences. "I did it partially for the religious experience, of course, but I did it because the church is another avenue for serving people who are needy, both spiritually and in other ways. I don't think I'll ever want to give that up.

"I feel that seeking social justice through the church is a spiritual expression," Norm adds. "However you do it, if you help people find meaning in their lives, then you find meaning in your own life. And it doesn't matter whether you're old or young, retired or still working."

CHAPTER FIVE

Reinvigorating Friendships

REUNION
Now thirty-five years later what's left?
Nothing I would recognize
and more important
nothing that would recognize me.
Even the memories are stale,
nurtured by people who don't know one another
but gather anyway and play golf and talk
about how old or how fat or how gray
we have become,
saying "remember the time" a hundred times
then when the times run out of memory
having nothing to talk about.
Yet we will gather again,

called and bound by something
we don't understand but feel anyway,
hoping that in one hotel or another,
at one bar or another,
on one golf course or another,
we will find it again
and be bathed in those feelings
we remember
of that other time and place. . . .

In partial answer to Sam Keen's question about where am I going and who is going with me, I rush to answer, "Friends." Friends are going with me wherever I go. That is, I hope they do. As close members of my family have died over the past two decades, my friends have become ever more important, almost like the new family.

An old proverb rightly refers to friendship as "the wine of life," but it is a wine that needs tending. Friendship requires mindfulness, hard work, and sometimes a commitment to reconciliation.

Some years ago, one of my closest friends and I were torn apart by a professional misunderstanding. At the time, I was about to move to another city; shortly afterward he also moved. We did not see each other or speak for over a year.

Then I accepted another job back in the original city and moved again. My friend wrote me a letter that began, "Despite the late unpleasantness, etc.," and suggested we talk and perhaps get together. The "late un-pleasantness" phrase was an in-joke between us because we both had admired Winston Churchill's use of it when describing World War II. In doing so, Churchill signaled his intention to look ahead, not back, in order to build a new future.

This is exactly what my friend and I wanted to do, and we did. We remain friends today. It is a deeply cherished friendship for many reasons, not the least of which is that after our split, we were both able to put aside our egos, forget the misunderstanding, and renew the relationship. I will forever credit him with making the first move toward reconciliation.

We were fortunate in that we had not been estranged so long that we lost common ground. Friendships can become rusty

> *Friendships can become rusty with neglect; they need the lubrication of contact and meaningful conversation, and, believe me, holiday cards once a year won't do it.*

with neglect; they need the lubrication of contact and meaningful conversation, and, believe me, holiday cards once a year won't do it.

Sometimes friendship can be renewed after many years, and sometimes it can't. Some of my most disappointing experiences since retirement have come when I contacted old friends after many years to find that we had grown apart. They were preoccupied with their present-day interests and concerns that were not in any way consonant with my interests and concerns. It's not that we felt ill will toward one another or fell into conflict or sharp disagreement about something. To the contrary, the get-togethers were cordial. It's just that the bonds of yesteryear's shared experiences were not enough to help us find common ground today.

The Beauty of Old Friendships

Yet old friendships remain, renewed and reinvigorated after an intentional effort to overcome geography or other circumstance in order to spend time together.

One of my most enduring friendships is with Sam Gore. Forty-seven years ago, I graduated from college with Sam. He and I then went through Air Force pilot training together, both getting our wings as jet fighter pilots. We went our separate ways, but about a year later, Sam was transferred to my base in Chaumont, France.

I got out of the Air Force; Sam stayed in. After 185 combat missions in Vietnam, he returned to civilian life and became an airline pilot.

Over all these years, we have remained best friends and in recent years have become even closer, focusing our association on two activities that have always bonded us: fishing and music.

When I talk about fishing, I don't mean the kind of wade-the-mountain-streams-and-find-the-wily-trout fishing so embraced by baby-boomers and celebrated in the popular media these days. That's a little too delicate for Sam and me. I mean a kind of fishing we used to call "meat fishing," the kind of fishing we depended on as boys to help put food on the table.

About twice a year, I go to Memphis where Sam meets me in his utterly disreputable van pulling a "meat fisherman's" boat, which no yuppie on Earth would ride in. Sam calls his boat *Death Wish*, but it's not as bad as it sounds. There's only a small leak, and we usually just get our feet wet.

By the time Sam arrives in Memphis, he has acquired a few hundred bait fish, small perch he either seines from his own pond or buys somewhere along the highway. One time his pond was flooded, and there was no good bait to be found in the shops, so Sam went by a pet store and bought all the good-sized goldfish they had. Those Mississippi River catfish must have thought they'd died and gone to heaven; they loved those goldfish.

We launch the boat into the Mississippi River several miles south of Memphis. Then we spend a few hours baiting and setting hooks. The hooks are rigged, ten or twenty to a line, on long lines, one end of which is tied to a tree along the bank, the other end tied to a large rock that we drop out in the river, thus stretching the line with its baited hooks out into the most likely looking water. This kind of water is described as "fishy looking."

After setting perhaps two hundred hooks, we reload the boat onto the trailer and go find ourselves some barbecue and beer. The next morning, we return to the river and "run the hooks," taking off the fish, if any, and rolling up the hooks for another day.

We usually catch several kinds of catfish, ranging from five or six pounds up to thirty pounds. A lot of people would call these big ugly fish, but my history is so tied to catfish that I almost think of them as distant cousins. (This does not prevent me from eating them, however.)

Understand that it is not catching fish that makes this such an important event for me. It is the doing of it, the method, the rhythm, the technique. It is the way the boat skims over the river; it's the huge tugboats and their barges of which we have to stay clear or be swamped by their wake. It's the waterbirds, the sandbars, the sun on the water, the fact that it's a mile across the river at that point; and of course, for me, it's the very mystery of the river itself, roiling in some places, brooding in others, calm and treacherous at the same time. Yes, it is a spiritual experience.

Another dimension to the friendship with Sam involves music. Sam is a fine jazz piano player; I'm a mediocre clarinetist. We've played music together in college and in the Air Force in France and now in a group called the Over the Hill Jazz Band. In addition to Sam and me are five other guys, some a little younger than we but not much. One is a doctor, another a judge, another a retired Air Force colonel.

The other members of the group all live in Mississippi, so I don't get to play with them very often, but for over a decade they've come to my home city and have played one or two nights at a local country club. I like to brag that we can play six hours without sheet music, without repeating a song, and we never play anything written after 1955.

This is good fun, of course, but it also is a connection with friends that binds us in ways that are not obvious. Music requires a communication that transcends words; an ensemble is a community in which each member contributes to the whole, the result of which sounds better than any one of the members playing solo. It simply creates something beyond what each person can do alone.

I HAVE YET another group of friends who, for eighteen years, have gathered every Columbus Day for a weekend retreat of good conversation, good food, and what can only be called spiritual exploration. My wife and I refer to this weekend as our "high holy holidays" because there have been times that we've felt suspended in the presence of the sacred as each couple told of the previous year's happenings.

In the past several years, some members of the group have managed to vacation together, and the same magic happens on a boat in the Greek Islands, aboard a barge in France, or in a hotel in Ireland. We see the world in a different way; it is not overstated to say we try to experience the spiritual essence of a place, but whether that essence is of the place or of our connection is impossible to say.

I recall a particular high point at one of our gatherings. Our host was describing an experience in Africa when, on a dark night, he was observing a pool of luminescent fish. When he looked up at the stars, then back again at the fish, it struck him that these lights were really not separated, and he described how he began to wonder where he fit among them. He paused, cupped his hands in front of his face—a casual gesture, I think— then looked across the dinner table to another friend, a highly regarded theologian, and asked, "So just what is worship?" The friend smiled, raised his hands in the same gesture, and said, "That's it. That's worship."

I was profoundly moved by the exchange; for the rest of the weekend we discussed the nature of worship and how it is possible to worship just by expressing our wonder at the world and our gratitude for being in it together.

The Power of Reunions

Reunions are something else again and can be very worthwhile events at which everybody can suspend their preoccupations and concerns of today and live for a while in the past with old friends, even if they are still friends only in the context of the reunion. For those few days, it's good to remember how things used to be, how close you once were to one another, how you thought those times would never end. It's even good to renew old pledges to spend more time together, to stay in touch, and so on. And, of course, retirement can make that connection more possible than it was when a job tied you to home and office.

I left active duty in the Air Force many years ago, at age twenty-six. At the time, I thought the pilots and their wives who were so much a part of my daily life at a small and remote air base in France would always be part of my life. I couldn't imagine how they would not be. After all, we'd endured inconveniences and hardships; we'd seen our comrades killed in accidents and had bid farewell to their widows and children; we'd spent many hours on alert not knowing whether we were going to war or not. These are intensely bonding experiences that, it seemed to me, would keep us always an integral part of one another's lives.

But it was not to be. Time and geography and circumstance separated us in more ways than we could have imagined, scattered us all over the world, and within a few years reduced us to Christmas card friends.

Then about twenty years ago, someone decided there should be a reunion of all the people who had served at that base between the years 1954 and 1959, at which time the base was transferred to the French. For one reason or another, I hadn't attended the reunions until three years ago. When I got the notice, I called several of my formerly closest friends and said, "If you'll go to the reunion, I will."

I was not prepared for the emotion of it. Oh, I expected to see a bunch of gray heads and bulbous bodies; I expected old war stories and laughs and toasts to one another and to old friends lost to accidents or the Vietnam War; I expected to be moved by some of the memories. But I was astonished by the emotional intensity of my response and by how deeply embedded the sheer power of that experience forty-some years ago had become.

Here are some notes I made at the end of each day:

The first day: There is something profoundly sad about being with these old warriors with their prostate problems, hearing aids, and paunchy middles. I keep seeing them as young men strapping on G-suits and parachutes and climbing into airplanes, returning later exhilarated from the mission, to join together in the officers' club or a barracks and drink, then sing their songs deep into the night, only to get up and fly again the next morning.

I've become obsessed by the mystery of time, the power of memory, the transcendent connections that make matters of politics or philosophy or religion irrelevant, that instead make us again as we were, young fighter pilots risking together our lives and fortune and sacred honor (to borrow a phrase) to do the job we were given to do and that we chose to do.

The first evening: The difficult thing is to connect these men with the fact that most of them are bona fide heroes. Most retired from the Air Force. Many flew in Korea and Vietnam; some flew in World War II, Korea, and Vietnam. These graying, paunchy old men have been prisoners of war, have been shot down and bailed out, have killed, have seen friends killed. Most are decorated to some extent; probably all who retired from the Air Force hold the Distinguished Flying Cross, and some hold Silver Stars. They chose to live the life of warriors, have fought the good fight, have been willing to die for what they believed in. And now, some stooped, some with chronic, killing diseases, have struggled their way back to this place to be among comrades, to remember other comrades come and gone, to gather in the glow of shared experience, to bask again in the community of pilots doing what pilots always do, flying with their hands the missions of yesteryear. And they know that this may be the last time, that they may never see each other again. But with pilots it was always so. Before every single mission. That, too, is part of it.

Midnight after the banquet: I sit here, eyes still burning from tears that came unexpectedly as I walked down the hall to my room. We had dinner at the Air Force Museum, surrounded by the airplanes we used to fly, then all returned to the hospitality suite. There was no booze left, no snacks, very little mix, but people appeared with bottles and mix and ice and somehow it multiplied, as with the loaves and the fishes, until we all had something to drink. There was really nothing left to say, no one left to greet. But we couldn't leave. We seemed to feel that if only we could have one more drink, tell one more story, the years and the wrinkles and the paunches and the gray hair would magically melt away and we would be back where we were forty years ago, at that little base in Chaumont, in the officer's club, celebrating once more the very fact of being there, alive, young, filled with expectation, and living an adventure we had never imagined would be ours.

We have agreed to do it again. Tomorrow morning, someone, we hope, will volunteer to host the next reunion two years from now. As I walked down the hall, however, I thought of Murphy and his fight now with cancer, and it hit me that he may not be alive two years from now. Nor may any of us. So I guess that's why the tears came. Now though I'm thinking once again that it was always like this with this group; we never knew when all of us would be alive together again. Not even the next day.

And it came to me suddenly that the reunion was not about keeping the old stories alive. We did not tell the stories to keep them alive; we told the stories to keep one another alive. Even the dead.

I SUGGEST THAT reunions of all kinds, from high school and college class reunions, to club reunions, to old-time hometown and church homecomings, offer just as fertile an opportunity for connection and meaning as did my Air Force reunion.

A close friend wrote to me last spring after attending his fortieth high school reunion. "I started not to go," he said, "because I figured I'd just see a bunch of old people and it would remind me that I'm getting older. But I was surprised. Everyone had aged, of course, but we didn't act like old people; we even got a little silly, the way we were in high school. It was fun. I didn't go there looking for anything, but I found it anyway."

A Time for New Friends

Retirement should not be only about old and enduring friendships. In fact, we often become too comfortable in the pattern of our friendships and their accompanying activities. We need something to break those patterns, to open us up to other people, other activities, and other possibilities. To be sure, as you've just read, old friendships are to be treasured and nurtured, but in some cases, they can also become predictable to the point of being deadening and boring. One of the great risks of retirement—and of growing older, for that matter—is the risk of becoming stale, of losing our zest for life, of settling for the same old everything because we're comfortable with it. You've seen people trapped in those attitudes, and I have, too.

Retirement is a perfect time for making new friends, a process that in itself can provide opportunities for

CONSIDERING A REUNION?

Here are some questions to ask yourself and some sources of information and help:

1. Think about why you want to get your military unit, educational class, work group, or other organization together. What do you hope such a meeting will accomplish? In other words, what's motivating you to have a reunion?

2. Take a trip down memory lane and the experiences you had with the people in your group. Look through photos, scrapbooks, and other correspondence and mementos of that time you all shared. What made that group and your experience together so special?

3. Do some historical research about the time in history when your group was together to fit your experience in a larger perspective. This step might also help you in your search for members you've lost touch with. Gather memorabilia and clippings to display at the reunion.

4. Think about the intangible gifts each member of your group would bring to such a gathering and ways you could best celebrate these gifts. Make these unique to your group and the experiences you shared.

5. Before you have the first reunion, list ways you can keep the reunions going. Share these with the other members at the reunion, and if the group decides to continue the practice, you'll be ready.

Good Internet Resources

http://dir.yahoo.com/Society_and_Culture/Reunions/ is an overall listing of resources with many links to other sites. It lists magazines and other research sites in the following categories: Birth Parent Searches, Camps, Companies, Families, Military, Schools, and World War II.

www.reunionsworld.com has resources for hosting high school class reunions and includes a military reunions link. They also offer reunion-planning advice.

www.military.com posts reunions by branch of the service. The Web site also has a search engine for finding old buddies and other reference materials.

Search google.com for companies specializing in planning and hosting reunions.

personal and spiritual growth as you learn about other people and, in turn, let them learn your story.

But how to go about it? You can't just go out on the street and say, "Hey, will you be my friend?" It requires a careful, deliberate, and intentional process that begins with the question "What kind of person do I want to be friends with?" And if you are to grow and learn from a new friendship, then the answer should not be "someone just like me."

Retirement is a perfect time for making new friends, a process that in itself can provide opportunities for personal and spiritual growth.

To begin, however, you can consider identifying people with common interests such as hobbies, clubs, church groups, and so on. This will put you in contact with people whose common interests could make them potential friends.

Think about friends you've had throughout your life at school, the workplace, church, and other places. Make a list of qualities you've always liked about those friends. Also list what made the friendships so special, then be mindful of those qualities when meeting potential new friends.

One good low-risk idea for widening your circle of friends immediately is to host a dinner or party where each guest brings one or two people you don't know.

You'll have the comfort of being with friends you do know but meet new people at the same time.

By all means, also consider developing contacts with younger people. It's important to make friendships with people younger than you; it's important for them to benefit from the wisdom of someone older, and it's important for you to hear young viewpoints. Most of the retired people I interviewed were quite passionate about maintaining friendships across a range of ages.

Give some thought to what knowledge, skills, and other gifts you could share with young people. Don't sell yourself short: Life wisdom is just what many young people need, just as you need their optimism and energy.

A great deal of personal and spiritual growth results from embracing other relationships that you've felt might be outside your comfort zone. Perhaps this is the time in your life to decide to reach out and try to become friends with someone of a group or religion or ethnic or racial background that you've never been friends with. Perhaps you've never had the opportunity, perhaps you've been uncomfortable with the thought, or perhaps you just haven't had time to explore outside your circle of existing friends.

There are many ways to go about finding new friends and acquaintances. But you may have to be bold about it, and you might have to put some effort and research into it.

Most newspapers list social and volunteer organizations that meet regularly. Shoppers also carry this kind

PEN PALS

Perhaps you'd like to do as many other people do and establish a pen pal relationship. The Internet is a rich resource for this, but a word of caution: Be wary of a pen pal who gets too personal or who seems to want to sell you a product or service or "let you in on a sure-fire stock deal" or something like that.

Try these pen pal sources: **www.internationalpen pal.com** and **www.pen-pals.net**.

of information. Your place of worship might have listings of groups of people from the church or those who use the building for meetings. Visit libraries and other public places that might have message boards about various groups and meetings. The possibilities are endless if you look carefully.

ARTHUR'S STORY

You Can Use Your Business Skills for the Rest of Your Life

Arthur Neis has never forgotten the day soon after he earned his master's degree when he asked his father to co-sign a note payable. His father, who at the time was hoeing weeds in the strawberry bed of his produce farm, said, "Well, you have all this education, but I don't know if you can hold a job or not." Says Arthur, "It was a real kick in the ass."

He has held a lot of jobs since then, and now as vice president, treasurer, and chief financial officer of a large company specializing in managing and providing services and living accommodations to retirement communities, he has probably proved all he needs to prove about his ability to hold a job.

But simply holding a job is not what Arthur devotes himself to. "Whether it's my job, personal relationships, or volunteer activities," he says, "the great imperative I feel is to add value."

"Added value" is one of those terms heard most commonly in reference to products or to manufacturing and other business processes, but Arthur applies it to all aspects of his life, and he expects to continue to apply it to his retirement life.

"I have never thought about retirement," he says, "yet I have always thought about retirement. I can remember in my twenties thinking, 'I've got to think about something other than this twelve-hour-a-day job.' I so often hear retirement as a point in time when there are massive changes in your life. I have retired dozens of times, going from position to position, leaving a board, leaving an organization. I just don't perceive that there's a point in time when you 'retire,' as if you turn off your mind. As far as I'm concerned, retirement will be just a matter of shifting the allocation of hours in the day. I don't have to get away from anything to go to something. In other words, I have always thought of my life after full-time employment in the context of where I am right now."

For Arthur, the road to where he is right now started with a strong sense of family. "When I was a kid, we were poor and didn't know it. Growing up in a little town in Kansas, next to the dirt, can either result in cynicism about everything or appreciation for the beauty of creation." Arthur's response was appreciation even though he has suffered losses.

His only sibling, a younger brother, died before he was fifty. In the fifth grade, Arthur met a friend who would later become his business partner for more than thirty years. Then the friend died, which created tumultuous times for the business and for Arthur personally.

Three years ago his wife died, another terrible blow and a disruption he had never imagined. "The death of my wife clearly interrupted a pattern but has, ironically, permitted me to shift away from being concerned that we had provided for ourselves and would never be a burden on others . . . to now thinking of legacy. You know, when we realize that we are not in control except for our own thought patterns and behavior, it really does simplify the world."

Arthur affirms that he is both emotional and spiritual, but he does not use the vocabulary of emotion and spirituality, whatever that vocabulary may be. "When I think of spirituality, I just don't know how to define it. My question is 'Do you feel it?' I think people who are spiritual are living way beyond themselves and conceptualizing way beyond themselves. By that, I mean they're always giving more to the space they occupy than they are taking.

"What bothers me about the word *spiritual* is that it has a lot of trappings and baggage. I hear the word so often misused in a negative context, to put down people who aren't 'spiritual.' I believe that all situations I find myself in, professional or personal, permit me to live beyond the immediate world and see the huge world out there. This allows me to integrate and not be as reactive; it also nourishes my desire to live in the beautiful world, particularly the world of fine art.

"When I'm in the theater or in Avery Fisher Hall [in New York City's Lincoln Center] and Kurt Masur steps to the podium, that's all there is in the world for the next two or three hours, almost like getting on a magic carpet and going somewhere. Wherever it takes me is where I want to go. But I'm not sure I'd call that a 'spiritual experience.'"

This from the man who is most comfortable doing something, particularly something in which he is adding value.

"Why is it necessary for me to perceive that I add value?" he asks. "One of the factors driving me is to be relevant wherever and whenever I am, to make a difference, to leave things better than I found them. Ludwig von Mises wrote that in every transaction between individuals there is revenue. Sometimes it's monetary, most times it's psychological, and we are always acting to be better off (as we perceive it) after the transaction than before the transaction. So you see, 'value added' is much more psychological than it is monetary.

"And how can we be relevant in the world without doing something, without action? Even in the most intimate of relationships, an action such as holding a hand or hugging is still doing something. For instance, when my business partner died, I saw his sister at the funeral. It was the first time she and I had been together in perhaps thirty years, and at that time we needed each other. We worked together through some tumultuous times, to salvage the business, to get it sold. We still exchange e-mails, send books to one another, and work to stay in touch. That's action, too.

"Not long ago, I spent a weekend in Los Angeles with a woman who grew up a few miles from me. We went to school together years ago. When I returned from Los Angeles, she wrote how much fun it was because she seldom has anyone to spend time with. That's also what I mean by adding value.

"Where does my drive come from? I really don't know. Perhaps it was the attention to personal living values and life that I first experienced as I grew up. Or maybe it's guilt at my successes and wanting to share, recognizing the difference between what I need and what I have might as well be shared in order to increase the total value around us. And how do you add value in personal relationships? I don't think you ever really know except in retrospect. You have to just keep going ahead, trying to be appropriate in all relationships."

Arthur has been active as a volunteer for most of his adult life, serving on boards of foundations and associations. In every situation, Arthur has asked himself, "Am I adding value?" He doesn't worry about how people perceive him as

"One of the factors driving me is to be relevant wherever and whenever I am, to make a difference, to leave things better than I found them."

long as he knows he has done all he can to add value. "I am who I am," he says. "I presume that how I'm identified depends on the value I may add to any moment with other people."

Still, he does find time in his life for experiences such as the concert in Avery Fisher Hall. As chairman of the board of the Alliance for Arts and Understanding, an international choral music program, he has spent time at the Abbey at St. John's in Minnesota. "I've had that same feeling I described at the concert while in the Abbey or walking in the cemetery at St. John's, or attending poetry readings, or listening to the chiming of the bells, and at the prayer services."

So how about retirement? "Who knows? There'll be a day when I'm not in this particular job. I am comfortable that whatever I do will be just as fulfilling. Perhaps the senior job corps or something like that. I have a list of things I want to do next. Top of the list is spending more time with family, more participation in the arts. And I've been thinking a lot about legacy."

Arthur says that the artistic director/executive director of the Alliance for Arts and Understanding has given him the opportunity to commission some music. "I'm at a point where I can do that kind of thing now, making sure that certain books get published and music gets written, and so on."

Then he pauses and says, "Just think, fifty years from now when no one ever heard of me, the music and literature will survive and will be there to be enjoyed by other people."

That's Arthur—planning to still be adding value long after he's gone.

CHAPTER SIX

Rekindling Old Intimacies, Discovering New Ones

IF YOU'RE NOT very well connected with your spouse before you retire, chances are that retirement will do nothing to strengthen the relationship and may very well exacerbate the disconnection. There are far too many stories of seemingly happy and stable marriages that became dysfunctional after retirement—so many stories, in fact, that the subject has become reliable joke material for comedians and humorists.

If before you retire you spend a lot of time at the workplace, then on weekends tend to do things separately such as play golf or go fishing or bowling with friends rather than your spouse, if you don't spend time in pleasurable activities together other than the most routine kinds of things such as watching television or eating, then you are likely headed for some marital problems after retirement. Or perhaps you're retired and are already experiencing these problems firsthand.

Either way, it's not too late to reinvigorate your relationship with the person you once felt would be your best friend, lover, and partner for the rest of your life. You don't have to settle for the kind of comfortable, predictable,

> It's not too late to reinvigorate your relationship with the person you once felt would be your best friend, lover, and partner for the rest of your life.

and—admit it—dull and boring relationships we so often read about and see in the popular media. And while there's something to be said for comfortable relationships and certain areas of predictability, there is nothing to be said for "dull and boring." (Conversely, if you're among those fortunate people who have a strong and growing marriage when you retire, then retirement gives you the time and opportunity to make it even better.)

You don't have to believe that nonsense about "mature marriages" being characterized only by habit and quiet desperation rather than an active and enduring love filled with romance, exploration, and personal and spiritual growth. And don't succumb to all the media-inspired stuff, some humorous, some serious, about being too old for romance, being too old for intense loving relationships, being too old to discover new aspects of your relationship.

Yet you don't just get up one morning and say, "Honey, let's be romantic and intense today." Reconnection and reinvigoration require a process that begins with the mutual recognition that your relationship needs renewed attention and then an agreement between you and your spouse that you *want* to reconnect. Without that recognition and that commitment, it won't happen. People who have serious problems are those who somehow think they're not going to have to work at it. They think they're just going to do more of the same, whatever it is. But what's clear is if you are going to avoid the trauma that so frequently results from the sudden togetherness of retirement, then the spouse must be at the top of the list of friendships to be reinvigorated and must be the most important friendship you have.

None of this is to suggest that you should never do things separately, that one can't play golf and the other play tennis or whatever the separate activity may be. That can be healthy, but the separate activities should never become more important than those things done together.

Your situation may be as simple as making the commitment to spend time in mutual interests that engage both of you, such as the mythological study group that Jeanne and Al Cahill attend, or the travel planning that John and Holly Clark do, or the humanitarian projects that Roy and Marilyn Reese take on. You could decide to learn something new together, to take a course, or to go someplace you've never been and to do it as a lone couple rather than as part of a group.

But understand that it may not be as easy as making the mutual commitment, and you may not be able to do this without help. You may benefit from pastoral or family counseling. You might be wise to seek couples or individual therapy. Many people feel there has to be a "problem" or some pathology evident in a relationship in order to benefit from therapy, but a more enlightened view is that a few sessions of therapy can help illuminate any latent issues and can help you develop a process for rekindling the interests and passions that brought you together in the first place.

There are also workshops and retreats designed specifically to help couples renew their intimacy; one of those may be just the thing to jump-start your relationship. They are not difficult to find. If you have friends, young or old, who have experienced such a workshop or retreat, don't be shy about asking them. That's a great source. Also look in the yellow pages under "Counselors, Marriage and Family," and "Retreat Facilities." If you are connected with a place of worship, chances are that will be an even better place to find these resources.

The Importance of Passion

Another cliché about aging and retirement has to do with romance and sex. Remember the Gertrude Stein

HERE ARE SOME INTERNET RESOURCES

Many organizations have Web sites discussing work-shops and retreats in their areas. Search on **google** **.com** for couples retreats; search also under the type of retreat you think you'd like such as spiritual, adventure, marriage renewal, transformational, and so on. If you want one associated with your religious faith, specify that as well.

www.passionatemarriage.com, run by the Marriage and Family Center in Evergreen, Colorado, offers many kinds of information and lists their workshops and couples retreats.

www.imagopartners.com offers "Getting the Love You Want" workshops, based on the work of Dr. Harville Hendrix in his book of the same name. Dr. Hendrix and his *New York Times*–bestselling book have been featured on the Oprah Winfrey show. His institute has a Web site covering a broad range of topics about relationships: **www.imagotherapy.com.**

Workshops for all kinds of couples, with descriptions and links, can be found at **www.menstuff.org /calendar/workshops/couples.html.**

www.wwme.org is the site for Marriage Encounter (ME) weekends presented by the Roman Catholic Church. The site lists other denominations that present ME weekends, plus related sites.

quote: "We're always the same age inside." And everyone has heard that "you're only as old as you feel."

Whichever cliché you recall on this subject, the fact is that you are not too old to look inside yourself and find again the youthful passion that propelled you into and throughout your courtship, romance, and early married years. Sam Keen has written that a life without passion is a life without real meaning, without texture, without diversity.

This is not to deny or denigrate in any way the quiet, wonderful, enduring, and deep love between people who've been a long time married. It is only to say that passion is an essential part of the life force, and you don't outgrow it. True, over the years you may have redirected your passion toward work, children, leisure activities, or volunteering, but retirement is the time you and your spouse can recapture at least part of it for yourselves. It's a time for bringing new romance into your life, perhaps a little late-life courtship, a chance to explore and deepen your most important relationship.

In my retirement I've heard all the aging-body jokes, and, indeed, I've met couples who admit that they never touch one another. I'm not talking only about sexual intercourse but am including such simple expressions of sensuality and sexuality as massaging the other's hands, or embracing, or holding hands.

Reinhold Niebuhr said, "Love is rejoicing in the otherness of the other." Part of that "otherness" in which we should rejoice is the body. If you are parents, yours are the bodies that participated together in the great creative miracle of birth; yours are the legs that walked crying babies in the middle of the night; yours are the arms that held and comforted children. And yours are the bodies that became a horsie for toddlers, that pulled red wagons, that played basketball and baseball and football and soccer, that rode bikes, that sat in hard seats in the high school gym or in the auditorium, that paced the floor outside a hospital room. Your bodies are part of everything you have ever done in your life.

Among the great and enduring mysteries is that we never outgrow the capacity to use our bodies for our own and others' pleasure and benefit, even though our bodies may not be the vibrant instruments they once were.

Physical intimacy is an important part of romance and should be an important part of marriage regardless of age. There's no quota of intimacy or sexual expression that we somehow use up along life's path; it continues to be available to us in one form or another. I know one just-retired couple who regularly rents a hotel room with a large soaking tub just so they can fill it with perfumed gel and take a bubble bath together. Sound frivolous? Maybe, but it definitely helps keep the romantic spark in their lives, and it shows.

The good news is that you don't have to wait until you retire to pay attention to this aspect of your relationships. And you shouldn't wait.

Physical intimacy as we age often flows better with increased emotional intimacy, so if it's been a while since you've talked with each other about anything besides bills and social obligations, reconnect first without worrying about physical intimacy. If you're not sure how to begin this process, try some of these suggestions. I offer them as ideas that might help you see each other in a new light and rekindle the spark.

All these activities have been proved effective in various venues, from couples retreats to classrooms. Some of them may sound silly, but if you approach them with a positive attitude, they can work for you, too.

Start with a very simple game at mealtimes that you may even have used to teach your children how to have good dinner conversations. Ask each other, "What was the worst part of your day? What was the best part of your day?"

Then make an iron-bound rule that you will regularly set aside time to talk about anything *but* everyday stuff—bills, chores, obligations, and so on. You can think of this as actually making a date to talk or do something you both enjoy—unless it's watching television or some other activity that eliminates conversation—even if it's only an hour or so at first. Write these dates on your calendar, and preserve them as you would any other important appointments. Plan subjects to talk about if that helps you be prepared.

Now, to help move you to the next stage of more or renewed intimacy, here are some additional ideas. For these you need to find a substantial period of quiet time, preferably an entire evening, when neither you nor your partner is distracted. In other words, don't try to squeeze these in between other obligations. Admittedly, some of these activities might seem forced at first if you're not used to being with each other in this way, but keep at it and you'll find great rewards.

1. Before your big evening, make a list of questions similar to these: If you were a color, what would it be? If you were an animal, what it would be? If you were a vehicle, what would it be? If you were an Olympic sport, what would it be? If you were a character in a novel, television show, or movie, who would it be? Be creative and come up with five to ten questions.

On the evening you've set aside, go through all the questions, writing down your answers separately as you go but *not talking about them*. Don't overthink them or take too much time to answer. Also, this is not a list of your favorite things but items or people that should most resemble how you see yourself. For example, your favorite color might be red and you wear it all the time, but you see yourself as a more subdued, laid-back person who likes to keep people at peace, so you're more like the color blue.

When you've answered all the questions, share your answers aloud. Make sure you tell each other why, and relate stories about why your answers have meaning for you. Listen with your heart to each other's answers and stories.

While this may seem like a kid's game at first, the power of this exercise is in getting you to think more metaphorically about yourself and your spouse, to visualize your life, to stretch your imagination. You may be amazed at the conversation this exercise provokes.

2. Start this one by both of you selecting several of your favorite pieces of music or CDs, enough to last an hour or more at a time. Sit together, hold hands, and listen to the music each of you loves. You can talk about why the music moves you or just be quiet as you let the music do what music does so well, which is to help you get beyond words.

3. Here's an old reliable idea: Rent classic romantic movies, and make a night of it. Put on attractive pajamas or loungewear, lower the lights or light candles, sip wine, and let yourself get into the mood of the movie. Comedies can work, too, believe it or not. The trick is in moving some part of the evening beyond the ordinary, like being in your pajamas or indulging in a huge bowl of popcorn or strawberries.

4. Light candles, sit facing each other, and breathe deeply. Slowly touch each other, starting with finger-tips—one at a time—then knees or toes, forehead, noses,

shoulders, gradually coming closer and closer to each other. Smile at each other—laugh if you feel silly—but keep touching each other tenderly.

5. As you go through your day, remember that almost anything can lead to physical intimacy if you honor each other and hold each other in your hearts. Working side by side in harmony to accomplish something like planting a flower bed, building a piece of furniture, or cooking a meal can heighten your awareness of your spouse and lead to physical expression of appreciation.

6. Remember that sometimes the simplest things can spark affection:

> Swing together on a porch swing.
> Have a nice dinner in a dimly lit restaurant, holding hands and touching knees under the table.
> Take an afternoon nap together.
> Sing old songs.
> Watch the sunset or sunrise.
> Take a drive in the country, and look at the moon and stars.

You may decide to try none of these suggestions. That's okay. There are no tricks or special techniques for regaining or intensifying the intimacy with your spouse. Success depends only on the two of you, your commitment to each other, your desire to be as close as possible, and your intention to turn that commitment and desire into action.

New Intimacies

What if you're single? Perhaps you're divorced, or, as is often tragically the case as people age, your spouse or partner has died. What then? You will have old friends, of course, and, as suggested by the previous chapter, you may find great fulfillment in pursuing new and interesting friendships. You may decide that's enough.

Still, there may come a time when you realize that a life alone is not how you want to live. It's unfortunate but true that many people in this situation dismiss the idea of romantic love in their lives. "At my age?" they ask themselves or others.

The answer should be "Yes, at your age." Before you reject the idea of romance and deeper intimacy, please understand that it is not too late to seek and find both physical and emotional intimacy in life regardless of your age.

> *It is not too late to seek and find both physical and emotional intimacy in life regardless of your age.*

In interviews, both men and women have told me that seeking such intimacy is so intimidating they've never tried. "I just wouldn't know what to do or how to behave," a fifty-five-year-old woman told me. A man asked, "What woman wants to be seen with an aging guy with a pot belly and thinning hair?"

INTERNET RESOURCES

Several Internet dating services match you specifically by locale, age, and a variety of other factors. Most charge a fee for a month's or more subscription. For example, **www.seniorfriendfinder.com**, **www.match.com**, and **www.kiss.com** have good reputations and take significant precautions to protect subscribers. Still, as with any Internet connection, I urge you again to be cautious and use good judgment; don't respond to questionable sales pitches or propositions of any kind. Use the old rule of thumb: If it sounds too good to be true, it is.

If You Need a Support Group

www.WidowNet.org has resources, message boards, and a state-by-state listing of support groups for widows and widowers.

www.divorcecare.org is the Web site for a series of support groups and seminars for people coping with divorce. The site also has a search engine for local groups and online resources.

www.parentswithoutpartners.org is the Web site for the international organization that provides resources and ways to find local chapters for single parents of all ages, for all reasons.

These fears are real, to be sure, and you must face them one way or another if you are going to allow yourself to embrace, receive, and enjoy all the companionship, intimacy, love—and, yes—sexual expression you're still capable of.

There is no single answer, no single technique, for preparing yourself for new intimacies. Some people need counseling or therapy as they think about this new part of their lives. There are singles groups of all ages. There are publications that can help. There are travel tours organized for singles, and not just for "swinging singles" but also for more mature people.

Many of the questions and suggestions in chapter 5 will help you here because the search for friends is a good way to meet people you'd like to be intimate with, so check those resources.

You can also try the old-fashioned way: Ask all your friends about single people they know and pester them to introduce you.

One retired man whose wife died shortly after retirement went so far as to place an ad in the personal section of a newspaper. This seemed curious and somewhat far-fetched to some of his friends because those ads are so often only attempts to make sexual connections. But he was willing to take the risk of disappointment or even embarrassment. He wrote a sincere and serious ad. It worked: He met a woman, a widow, and, after an appropriate courtship, they are now happily married.

Another man of my acquaintance was divorced about a year ago. He has since connected with a woman who also was divorced. Both of them, in their midfifties, talked with me about the process. A particularly troubling issue, as it seems to be for many middle-aged and older people, was the one of body image.

Ann (I've changed the name) says, "Just look at all the women in magazines and on television. Young, young, young. And skinny. The whole fashion industry has convinced women like me that love and sex are only for the young and slim. In my mind I know that's nonsense, but psychologically it's very intimidating."

Dan (I've also changed his name) adds, "It's the same for men. All the rippling abs and bulging biceps. I finally had to just look at myself in the mirror and say, 'Damn it, Dan, somebody out there who looks a hell of a lot worse than you do is having fun, falling in love, and having sex. You ought to be able to do it, too.' Still it was difficult. What do you do? I couldn't go to bars and try to pick up women."

Ann and Dan met through mutual friends, but it took a while before Dan had the courage to propose a date. So what did they talk about on that first date? "Mainly," says Ann, "we talked about how difficult it was to be single in this world at our ages. Then we just had a very straightforward talk about the problems and about our fears and concerns.

"Then," she says, smiling, "later when I was more comfortable, I started flirting with him. I would do all

133

the stuff I used to do—touch his hand when I was making a point, look deep into his eyes. It made me feel I was in school again."

"I loved it," says Dan. "It was a shot in the arm. This may sound too macho, but it did make me feel like a man again, and I'd sorta lost that feeling."

"Then on the second date," Ann continues, "I just came right out with it. I told him I was scared to death at the thought of being sexually intimate. I couldn't even imagine taking off my clothes and getting naked with a man."

Dan admitted the same fears, and they spent the second date putting all their fears on the table and discussing them. Which is one of the lessons of this story.

Other lessons: You can flirt again. You can make yourself attractive again. You can reintroduce into your life some of the characteristics that made being young so exciting. Remember that none of this is reserved for the young.

Sam Keen has written that the greatest purpose of life is to love and be loved. Of course, he's talking about all kinds of love, but I believe that romantic love should not be relegated to a mere phase of life because romantic love is a great catalyst for other kinds of love. It is often romantic love that really opens our young eyes for the first time to the needs and desires of someone else, a lesson that then applies to family and children and neighbors and the less fortunate. And for older people, romantic love can become a catalyst for seeing the world as new again. And that, in itself, is one of the most life-affirming things you can do.

MORE OF PAT'S STORY

If You Have to Adjust to Life Alone

Life without a spouse or partner is an ever-present possibility in our lives, and it becomes even more likely—or almost certain—during retirement years. Sometimes people connect with a new partner; sometimes they choose not to. It would trivialize the subject to write about the impact of sickness and death as if it were a journalistic event rather than a life event, but at the same time, it is a subject to reflect on in any consideration of retirement.

Pat Barrentine (see her full story, page 36) had to face life alone after forty-two years. She wrote about it in August 1995 and has given me permission to extract the following from her essay:

> I wake. Look at the clock. It's 2:05 A.M. and you're not here. After forty-two years, your side of the bed is empty. I'm alone for the first time in my life. Sounds I'd ignore with you by my side seem louder—more mysterious. I listen hard, needing to identify their source.
>
> To sit alone at dinner without you to hold hands with in meditation is the hardest. I light the candles and set a nice table. You died in the winter so dinner is always after dark. The dark increases my sense of isolation. I use a lot more electricity. I need more light. I'm missing yours.

If I want a fire in the wood stove, I carry the wood, tend the fire. So many reminders of your absence. The little things you did without being asked. I rebel at doing maintenance—even things I can do. I call someone to fix things for me. I need to feel cared for.

My work is as demanding as it was the day I took you to the hospital. The pressure of it protects me from feeling the loss—part of the time.

In the midst of my sadness comes an unexplainable sense of peace and joy. I feel it deeply. Surely knowing that it's only your body, not your essential Self, that died helps. I treasure and build on that joy.

In three months, I travel to a work-related conference. My first step out. I welcome good conversation with interesting people. Two months after that conference, I attend a week's seminar and come home knowing it's time to give up part of my work, even though it brings me prestige and a great sense of competence. Hard to let go, yet I do. It's time. The relief I feel in turning it over confirms the rightness of my decision.

Planning another trip focuses my need to give up the rest of my work. I cannot come home to someone else's deadlines. So I fire myself. Tell clients I have to take time out. For how long, I have no idea. It's been almost two years and I won't go back to the same work.

Alone for the first time, new and exciting possibility stretches out in front of me. I can create my future any way I want. An awesome realization. I'm watchful. I don't want to create a new version of the past. It's not easy to discard patterns ingrained for so many years.

As my world expands, I travel to Mexico, Bali, Singapore, Greece, Switzerland, and many parts of the United States.

My time is my own. My life is my own. I struggle to bury my well-nurtured Puritan work ethic and find I can read all day leaving "important" things undone. I've retrained myself, given up old compulsions and habits. Reading all day is one of the gifts of being alone.

I fight feeling left out of activities, and come back to seeking purpose in this time. My friendships with women deepen. I need connection and caring. New friendships slowly form. I discover that to be alone is not to be lonely. The two do not have to go together. I treasure my solitude. In fact, I guard it. That I now welcome and cherish aloneness amazes me. Time to myself is a great gift. I drive on long trips, explore new cities, go to movies or out for breakfast alone. If I want company, I invite friends for dinner and enjoy cooking.

Your gentle hands no longer caress me. I need to be touched and get massage and chiropractic, do yoga. All help me release old patterns and energy blocks. My diet changes naturally. As I listen to my body, it willingly gives up most meat, favoring more vegetables.

The house we built has changed. A painting called *Joy* hangs over my bed. I buy paintings from close friends—*The Golden Fish, Blue Moon Dancer, The Gift.* Each represents a stage in my transformation though I don't recognize that when I get them. Photos from my travels replace old family pictures.

There have been two and a half years of changes. Do I still miss you? Of course, but I don't grieve. I celebrate your new journey and my own. The timing is always perfect if I can but find the gifts life offers me. One of those gifts is that we had no unfinished business—no regrets for words unsaid, life un-lived. We didn't put life off for an uncertain "someday."

Being patient as the next stage of my life unfolds is often hard. I so want to have an answer when someone asks, And what do you do? The truth is, I do whatever I choose to do, but that sounds smug and self-serving. Yet that's what I must have the courage to do—to follow my own heart in each moment knowing other gifts await me. (© Pat Barrentine, August 1995. Pat Barrentine is editor of *When the Canary Stops Singing: Women's Perspectives on Transforming Business* (Berrett-Koehler, 1993) and former editor of *World Business Academy Perspectives*. A mother of three and grandmother of five, she lives in the historic Gold Rush town of Nevada City in California.)

PART THREE

Time for Those Who Need You

Service is the rent we pay for being alive.

—Marian Wright Edelman

WE ARE ALL connected to the world in ways we don't even understand or don't even think about. We can't get up in the morning, take a shower, brush our teeth, and get dressed without those actions having touched in some way perhaps thousands of other people who were involved in producing the products we use. Most of those connections are beyond our personal control, and neither the people we touch nor we ourselves would be able to identify a personal or spiritual dimension to that contact. But it's there nonetheless. There are other connections to be made, intentional ones, over which we do have control and from which both we and the people we touch can derive enormous benefit. This section is about those relationships.

Among all the people interviewed for this book—and I emphasize *all* of them—there is one value they hold in common: service to others. Some serve through their churches, some through civic and charitable organizations, and some individually without organizational ties.

Of course, it's not uncommon for employed people to do volunteer work with service organizations as board members involved in policy and governance; it's less common for them to be in the trenches, doing the hands-on work.

I recall my first year in a large corporation when I got tapped to head the United Way campaign in the company. "This will look good on your résumé," my boss told me.

Serving in order to build a résumé is a lot different from serving in order to create a life of meaning and personal growth. I won't question the value of any service, but in the context of planning a retirement of spiritual growth, it's important to focus on the deeper meanings of service and the values on which service to others is based.

These values are compassion, humility, and generosity.

Compassion, the essential virtue of a kindhearted life, is no more than allowing the emotion of love to have free reign in our lives. Compassion, which can be aroused quickly, is often difficult to maintain; it is a great virtue precisely because it is not an easy one. Without vigilance, we can become convinced that the hard work of compassion is not worth the effort. Often this happens because the recipients of our compassion "don't seem to appreciate it."

Which leads to humility. *Humility* is the inward version of respect; that is, *respect* is humility manifest in our attitude toward others. But humility goes deeper than our relationship with others. True humility is the constant realization that no human being can ever be perfect and that we must all fall short of what we should be. Thus, we are prohibited from becoming self-satisfied and judging others, even judging their reaction to our kindness. As Confucius said, "To have faults and not to try and correct them is to have faults indeed."

The value that puts compassion and humility to work is *generosity*. A generous spirit is the mark of a person who is spiritually very evolved. Such a person has no concern for reward or recognition and seeks only the opportunity to be of service.

> *In creating a retirement life of spiritual and personal growth, the question is not whether to allocate time and energy to service but only to determine how much time and energy to allocate to it.*

143

The chapters in this section offer stories of people who serve the community through organizational work and those who choose to serve one person at a time.

Consider this: People of faith may have their religion-based beliefs about immortality. That's for each of us to determine individually. But I do know that our guaranteed chance at immortality comes from what we have done to help other people.

In creating a retirement life of spiritual and personal growth, the question is not whether to allocate time and energy to service but only to determine how much time and energy to allocate to it.

MARTI'S STORY
From Work to a "Calling"

Sometimes you have to wait until after retirement to have the time and emotional energy to seek and find your calling, because a calling is not usually part of the money economy, where the paycheck is financial, but rather of the grace economy, where the paycheck is spiritual.

Marti Sivi speaks with gratitude of her spiritual paycheck. "It's the compensation I get for giving back in some way to society," she says, going on to explain that her quest for God and for spiritual growth led her finally to prison. But not as an inmate. Here is her story:

"My whole life I have sought to find God," she begins. "When I was a little girl, I asked my mother where was God. When she said she didn't know, nor did anyone else, I remember thinking, 'Well, why is everybody doing all kinds of things every day instead of trying to find out?' I couldn't believe people were shopping, talking, making money, et cetera, without being preoccupied about finding God. I have looked for God everywhere in my life. I wanted certainty; I wanted hard facts. I wanted to know where the manual was for human relationships if God existed. Why did He just leave us here with nothing but our curiosity?"

In the early seventies, Marti joined the immigration of young Jews to Israel after the Six-Day War. She lived on Kibbutz Shefayim. She worked as a travel agent there (and later in the United States), got married and pregnant there. Her girls are now thirty and twenty-seven years old.

Back in the United States, Marti got a degree in criminal justice, though she has not worked directly in that field. Since she was five years old, she has worked in the theater wherever she's lived, always keeping that as a volunteer activity—a "hobby," never a profession.

"I was tempted to go professional only once," she says. "In San Francisco, when *Hair* premiered, if I'd had an equity card, I'd have taken off my clothes in a minute to join that show. But I had to pass it up.

"I'm intuitive by nature," she says, "and all my life I've sensed some connection with the greater universe out there. I've always told my kids to get to the point where you can see a door opening. In making choices, meditate on them, get quiet, and wait until you can sense the right thing to do. I've never regretted anything, even painful things, because I always walked through the doorway. I think I was born with the ability to sense the doorway and the right choices."

She describes the process as an internal dialogue between her and God. "I don't mean to make this sound like I talk directly to God, but I sense the connection. I don't get words. It's all visual, like a visual dialogue. It hasn't exempted me from making mistakes, but, on the other hand, I never look at anything as a mistake. I feel that everything I've been or done has led to the gratefulness of what I'm doing now."

And what she is doing now started with a prison doorway. She is putting her criminal justice knowledge and her theater background together to continue her quest for spiritual growth as a compassionate volunteer in a women's prison. Her work: producing and directing plays using only inmates as stagehands, prop and costume people, and actors.

As reported in *Bars and Stripes*, the newsletter of Criminal Justice Ministries, it all began when Marti was invited to an interfaith forum at a state correctional institution for women. She asked the chaplain about the women's emotional conditions. The answer: often depressed and suicidal.

Marti and the chaplain then agreed that drama classes could possibly be cathartic. So they made a proposal to prison officials.

The administration did not welcome the idea, and it took over a year to convince them to give it a test. In August 1998, the project began. Thirty women signed up to simply attend a script-reading class. Marti's deep hope was that eventually she could build self-confidence in the fractured women she met; in addition, she saw her prison classes as a creative outlet for the hopeless boredom of prison life.

For the first play Marti chose the female version of Neil Simon's *The Odd Couple*. It took only one class for the women to become so excited they wanted to actually perform the play. It required another two months for the administration to give additional permission for that.

Marti realized almost immediately that this was part of her spiritual journey, her search for God. "I had found support groups in the sixties and politics in the seventies. I joined my synagogue and tried to believe that ritualistic prayers could bring God closer, yet I still felt alienated. But God has never been closer to me than when I started working with women in prison."

For Marti, this turned into the calling she had been seeking all her life, and now, with her children grown and the rest of her life ahead of her, she has been able to devote herself to it. But not without some problems along the way. She had recurring struggles early on with the prison administration. They didn't want the women to wear wigs for fear they'd try to disguise themselves and escape. They didn't want the correction officers (guards) to watch the shows for fear the women would be seen as "too human." There were times that some of the cast members were restricted because of behavior, and once the whole cast voted to delay a show until after the star got out of "the hole"—solitary confinement.

Some personal issues for Marti also arose. "When I started this endeavor, it was only to bring theater into a facility that had a void. It was always structured 'for them.' On the first performance that fell on Yom Kippur, my husband told me not to go. 'If you go,' he said, 'I'd be afraid that God is going to punish you. Yom Kippur is a holy day. You should be in synagogue praying.' It was his interpretation of God, and I resented both of them."

She went to the play.

Since that time, the women inmates, under Marti's guidance as producer and director, have performed seven plays, including two premieres, one of them entitled *Mother's Day in the Holding Tank*, which is now being performed by a professional theater group in New York.

Marti's spiritual paycheck comes in many forms and at many times, but perhaps her experiences with two former inmate members of her theatrical troupe say everything that needs to be said about the rewards available to someone who holds service to others as a focal point of life.

Marti tells the stories: "I got a call from a woman who had been in my second show. She had been out on parole for a year and a half and wanted to meet with me." (Marti also managed to get an exception to a rule that had previously forbidden inmates to contact counselors or other caregivers after release from prison.)

"Cindy was cast as a methamphetamine addict in *Mother's Day in the Holding Tank*. At the time I cast her, I had no idea that her crime had been exactly that. She kept it from me until the very end of the play.

"We met at a restaurant. She looked good physically. She told me she was working at the Marriott Hotel and was grateful they had given her a second chance at life. She told me that in the time she spent in prison she was exposed to anger management classes and drug classes. She was asked to write a diary and interact with counselors. But she said that none of it found her; she was still bitter and lonely.

"She said she came to drama class just to busy herself with something until she left the prison. But when she was cast, she started to take on old feelings of addiction and anger. Her roommates told her to quit the play because she was becoming difficult to get along with, but she continued to force herself to work through all the feelings that were stored up inside. She said to me, 'When you go to prison, your soul leaves your body. That's the way they want it to be; it's easier to control. But when I came to the play, it was the beginning of the way back. I found my soul again.'

"We sat there crying. She told me of her past life for the first time. The rapes, the loss of children, the distrust of others who wanted to help. The play changed that for her, she said. She saw herself in a different way for the first time.

"She had come to the class tough and aloof. After six months, she said she saw how she had been on drugs and she reenacted what it looked like. It scared her, but she did it and got a standing ovation from five hundred inmates at the last performance.

"After she got out on parole, it was a year and a half before I heard from her again. She told me that she still has the playbill from the show, framed on her wall, and she looks at it often to know that she can do things in life that she never thought she could."

Marti is even more inspired by the story of Diana, a woman who had been an abused wife with seven children at an early age. When Marty met her, Diana was fifty-six years old and in prison for a crime she'd committed in submission to a violent man.

"She didn't want to read for a part," says Marti. "She told me, with eyes downcast and a halting delivery, that she didn't graduate high school, wasn't comfortable in front of people, even talking, but wanted to be in the class in some way."

Marti decided to have her do props, which mostly would involve hanging around, listening as the others started to learn their parts, then, closer to the show, working with Marti to decide what would be on the stage. No pressure. The play was *The Odd Couple*.

It was one of those times when things fell apart. "I got my dose of the reality of theater in prison: My lead actress was sent to solitary. Two weeks later, several more were sent. We needed some new people to take parts to be able to do this show at all. The whole project was on the line.

"One part in particular was the very humorous role of a man named Manolo Costesuelo. He was the upstairs neighbor of 'Olive and Florence,' the odd couple, and he had a monologue about life in the United States, as opposed to life in 'Ebana, Espana.'

"I asked Diana if she would consider taking the part. She was petrified, but I promised to work with her. To be honest, I didn't know how it would turn out, but I wanted her to know that I believed in her. We worked on her projection, her timing, everything, for four months.

"When the curtain went up, I stood in the back just barely breathing. This was an inmate audience, for the first time seeing other inmates performing a show. When the curtain went up, there was a roar from the audience, as they jumped up and gave a five-minute ovation before the first lines even came out! My group looked like deer in the headlights. I'd never seen this happen in theater before.

"When Diana's monologue came, she was incredible. She spoke with a strong, clear voice. And she was funny. It began, 'Mi nombre es Manolo Costesuelo, and I come from Ebana, Espana.' Her timing was impeccable, holding for laughs as we had practiced. When the curtain closed, I went backstage, and here were all the cast surrounding Diana, applauding her alone.

"She was crying with happiness. For the woman who told me that she had never had a woman friend in her life, to be experiencing all these women applauding her and telling her how wonderful she was, was overwhelming to see.

"When she was paroled, she had wanted to be in the next show because, as she said, 'It was the first time anyone had ever said I did something good.' She said it was the best thing that had happened to her. Then we said good-bye."

Two years later, Marti's phone rang at 10:30 P.M. She answered. A voice said, "Mi nombre es Manolo Costesuelo, and I come from Ebana, Espana."

After the laughter and the greetings, Diana told Marti that she finally had her children back, had divorced the man who had instigated her crime, and was off welfare. She called to tell Marti not only that she had a job but also how she got it.

She was interviewing for a telemarketing job, and the potential employer said, "Since you have to be on the phone a lot, we would like you to talk about yourself, so we can see how poised you can be."

Diana didn't want to talk about prison, so said she'd rather not talk about herself. "But we need to hear you speak," the future boss said. At that point, two other members of his staff joined the interview.

So Diana told the story of the play and her part in it, then closed with her monologue, "Mi nombre es Manolo Costesuelo . . ." The people applauded, and she was hired on the spot.

Marti is almost in tears as she tells these stories. "There are more Dianas and Cindys in every show I do up there . . . I truly believe I am the fortunate one to be able to watch these miracles of self transpire. Working with these women has given me the most spiritual moments I have had in my life, and I can only say that I feel

God's love and power as I am up there. My life has become so rich that there is never a bad day I can have. For women who can overcome such obstacles and go onstage with all the pain that every day can bring in prison, my respect is overflowing.

"I think of all the women I have worked with. In every one of them I see a kind of light. It is the light of potential that has been buried but it's still there, waiting to get out, waiting for someone to acknowledge it. As Cindy and Diana told of finding 'the light' in this program with me, it hit me that I have also found God in each and every face of the women I have grown to love there.

"Surely God is everywhere in our world. But it is still more illuminating for me to feel God's presence inside the prison walls. I wonder if spirituality in captivity resonates more? Did the inmates in that prison cross my path to help me, or vice versa? Probably both, and for that I am thankful every day."

CHAPTER SEVEN

Serving the Community

ONE OF THE things that most Americans don't realize is the degree to which our people's devotion to volunteerism is unique in the world. Other countries simply don't depend on volunteers the way we do. That is not to say that citizens of other countries don't work in community service; it's just that we do it to a far greater degree than anywhere else.

We seem to feel that helping others is just something that we do naturally. Author and spiritual leader Ram Dass has written, "[Helping] . . . is the instinctive response of an open heart. Caring is a reflex. Someone slips, your arm goes out. A car is in the ditch, you join the others and push. A colleague at work has the blues, you let her know you care. . . . You live, you help."

In the United States, this instinct to help has produced literally thousands of community service organizations dedicated to causes of all kinds, from the arts, to health and disability, to education and the environment. So chances are that if you have not already been involved, you will be.

In a retirement of meaning, the question is not whether to do community service but rather the nature of that service. A lot of us have served in one capacity or another in volunteer organizations almost as an adjunct to our careers. Our motivations were not ignoble in that we saw community service—again, unlike in most other countries—as part of the obligation of a successful person in society.

> *You've probably worked all your life to achieve your idea of the good life after retirement. Service to others also gives you the chance to achieve a life of goodness as well.*

So there was certainly nothing wrong with community service as part of a professional life, but as you leave a career, you have the opportunity to bring another consciousness to the process of serving others: the opportunity to put aside any thoughts of what this work may do for you and, instead, embrace fully what it may do for others. You've probably worked all your life to achieve your idea of the good life after retirement. Service to others also gives you the chance to achieve a life of goodness as well.

How Do You Begin?

I think it's fair to say that most people are drawn into community service either through intense interest in a cause or because someone they respect asked them to be involved. I've done both.

One of my sons was stricken with epilepsy in 1967 when he was seven years old. I was as ignorant about epilepsy in those days, as was 95 percent of our population. But it became clear in a hurry that people with epilepsy were not getting a fair shake. They were still classified by some as "having fits." They were disadvantaged in education and in many normal activities such as driving a car. In some states, sterilization was still authorized, and in others they were prohibited from marrying. So I became involved on the national board, later becoming president of the Epilepsy Foundation of America. It was good work with a worthy cause, and I learned more and was given more by far than I gave.

I've served on other boards simply because I was asked by a friend or colleague, once again learning more and gaining more than I gave.

The most important gift from all these activities was the opportunity for me to give without any expectation of reward. I loved my profession and my job and felt them to be noble and societally valuable endeavors; still, the business fundamentally involved selling things to people. On the other hand, the volunteer activities were all about giving, a whole different way of interacting with the people served by the organization. My volunteer activities have continued seamlessly into retirement life, still providing the opportunity to use my talents for the benefit of others.

Elizabeth Hawkins retired from her job as a clerk-cashier with a florist and immediately knew that she wanted to stay active and productive. She began volunteering in the office of her church, then became the church's volunteer coordinator of services for people living in homeless shelters.

"The church was happy for me to take this on," she says, "and it not only gave me something helpful to do but gave me a level of responsibility I'd never had before."

A CEO who thought he'd be with his company forever but who took early retirement as a result of dissatisfaction with his boss brings his senior management skills into retirement life, not in the service of profit but in the service of poor people in another country.

Vic (who did not want his full name used) went to Bolivia three times last year, trying to find a way for businesspeople to connect with poor people who want to do business. These, of course, are the skills he honed in his years as an executive.

"I have connected with a group of people in Bolivia who need to find a way to market their products," he says, "and I'm now working in the Midwest area to try to find a way to distribute and market their products here. This could help four or five hundred women. And the great thing is that when the women make the money, it helps the families directly. A little money goes a long way in these communities."

Another manager, unexpectedly early retired from a major West Coast electronics company, says that his lifetime of work and play included volunteer activities that proved to be most important in his transition. He has an MBA and an undergraduate degree in engineering but does not specifically seek to use that background.

"I do whatever they ask me to do at these organizations," he says. "I'm very comfortable stuffing envelopes or delivering meals or clothing to homes. It makes me more thankful for what I have.

"Unfortunately, I worry that a lot of young people these days want to be in a volunteer organization only if they can be vice president of this or that. I try to avoid organizations that focus on career building or attracting people who just want to put board work on their résumés."

Larry Brown (he did not want his real name used) was a carpenter and house painter who after retirement thought he'd never do that kind of work again. Now he volunteers his skills for all kinds of community service projects, many through his church. He has traveled to Mexico on a "Habitat for Humanity–type project" and recently worked with a group to help fix up a house for a Bosnian immigrant family. He often finds himself as foreman of the work crew. "A lot of the volunteers mean well and work hard, but somebody needs to tell them what to do and how to do it," Larry says. "That's where my experience comes in."

Who, What, and When

In choosing an organization or an area of volunteer activity, the first question should be "What do I care about?" Start with a category such as the arts, a health agency, a disability group, a poverty relief organization, a homeless families shelter, a domestic abuse support group, an environmental group, a historical preservation group, an employment training organization, a rehabilitation center, or a home for the elderly.

The list could go on and on, but I suggest that somewhere within the question of "What do I care about?" you'll find yourself answering another question: "Whom do I care about?" This is an opportunity to follow your heart and to focus on the causes and the people who most engage your concerns and your compassion.

The next question is "Where will I find the time?" Don't make the assumption that any of these involvements require a lot of time. These groups and organizations are abundantly grateful for whatever time you can devote to them, and they will gladly accommodate your schedule.

Having worked in many different kinds of nonprofit groups, I suggest that you pick a few and give a little time and effort to each before fully embracing one. The good thing about volunteering is that you get to decide where you can make the greatest contribution and what that contribution will be. Be warned, however, that once you begin to give of yourself in these ways, you will undoubtedly find that more and more of your time seems to open up and become available.

The last question is "What can I do?" You probably have more knowledge and skills than you realize. Be rigorous in making an inventory of those things you've mastered not only in your work but in your hobbies and leisure activities. All of it may come to bear in your volunteer activities.

One approach, as you have read earlier, is to continue doing what you've been paid to do, only now do it pro bono. Become a secretary or volunteer at

> *There's no limit; if you have skills, there's a place to use them in the service of others.*

your place of worship; offer clerical services at your local women's or family shelter; teach a class in how to put a résumé together; drive for Meals on Wheels; demonstrate

SOURCES OF HELP

There's a comprehensive Web site that's perfect if you're not sure where you want to volunteer or how much you want to get involved. Called Volunteer Match (**www.volunteermatch.org**), it lists volunteer opportunities that have been requested by nonprofits in your own area. You search by ZIP code. (Mine, in Des Moines, Iowa, listed eighty-two opportunities one day.) These can be events or ongoing projects that cover a wide range of needs, so you can pick and choose according to your skills, time, and commitment. The site also has links to several national organizations.

On the local level, call your United Way agency, an umbrella organization for various nonprofit organizations in the community. Some have volunteer centers that act as a clearinghouse of agencies, schools, and any organization looking for volunteers. The United Way posts a description of the activity, the application requirements, and information for

arts and crafts projects at a nursing home. There's no limit; if you have skills, there's a place to use them in the service of others.

you to follow up with the individual agency. The national Web site is **http://national.unitedway.org**.

Another good place to look is at your place of worship. Many if not most churches have their own programs, plus many of them encourage organizations to keep them informed about volunteer needs.

Also be open to trying new things outside your comfort zone. Perhaps you've always wanted to be involved in theater. Volunteer at a children's theater, or even stage amateur productions for elderly people or at homes for people with disabilities. The level of accomplishment is not as important as the desire to bring something new and unexpected to people whose lives are constricted and limited in many ways. The benefits for them are immeasurable, and you are given the opportunity to grow and to learn something new at the same time.

Never forget that the greatest and first beneficiary in this life of goodness will be you yourself.

ROY AND MARILYN'S STORY

The Caring Triangle—
Service, Travel, Relationship

Roy and Marilyn Reese have a Gertrude Stein quote framed on their kitchen wall: "We are always the same age inside." This reminds them not to dwell on the past but to look ahead and maintain the focus they bring to a life of meaning through service to others.

Roy insists that "our retirement is not one big humanitarian project," but it seems that way to the people who know and admire Roy and Marilyn. Their activities on behalf of others are not flashy, and they're not done for public accolades. In fact, the Reeses are such unassuming people that I feared they'd be reluctant to let me tell their story.

Both serve or have served on the local food pantry, the Child Abuse Prevention Council, and several other humanitarian organizations, as well as in programs at their church. Plus, they have created opportunities for service to individual people. For instance, a young female journalist from Thailand lived for two weeks in their home while studying practical journalism under the auspices of the Iowa Peace Network.

They welcomed as a houseguest a young man from Nigeria who was in the United States at a conference to encourage peace between Christians and Muslims. Roy was particularly drawn to the young man because, as

Roy explains, "At home he has no electricity, no water, no indoor toilet."

Then, pausing, Roy smiles, "It reminds me of years ago on our farm in southern Iowa. My parents were tenant farmers with no electricity, indoor toilets, or running water until I was a junior in high school. We walked through the fields to a one-room school with some of our teachers having only two years of training.

"These may be some of the factors that influenced me to help others, both here at home and in countries around the world. Can I help our houseguest from Nigeria? I hope so."

Whereas some couples deliberately set about to do things separately, to have time alone, and to define separate lives for themselves, even though still deeply connected, Roy and Marilyn are almost the opposite. "I won't say we operate as a team," says Marilyn, "but there are very few major projects where we aren't both involved. Of course, this may present a transition problem when one of us dies, but I feel the closeness of our joint projects, and everyday living is far superior to individual activities."

Not that they could have—or would have—planned their health problems, but both had successful cardiac bypass surgery a few years ago.

"This really put us in high gear planning for our future," Roy says. "People tell us they don't have time to go on work trips or vacations. Our answer is to list goals and prioritize just as you do in your business life. We take our top choices and block out time on the calendar, just as we would a doctor's appointment or any other engagement. This could be six months or a year ahead, but it still allows us to keep that time free of other activities."

In addition to their engagement in their hometown, Roy and Marilyn have traveled with their church youth choir to Europe; worked at a youth lodge and school after a hurricane in Hawaii; cleaned, repaired, and remodeled a school for retarded children in Moscow; and two years later did repair and construction work at a home for elderly women in Moscow.

Though they consider these activities extensions of their spiritual life, they are reluctant to define that term precisely. *"Spiritual*—nine letters with all kinds of meanings," they say. "On the island of Kauai, a native Hawaiian had us hold our hand on a good-sized rock half buried in the ground, to feel the spirit. Off the coast of Alaska, natives came aboard our ship and told of birds with special names and meanings. Deep in the Egyptian desert, our guide explained walls painted with ancient pictures and symbols. Our Native American Indians listen to the wind and watch the sun and moon for guidance."

Then Roy adds, "I'm convinced that the *babushkas* that we helped build housing for in Moscow were the primary force that kept the people of their country together during the seven decades of Communist rule. And these are just some of the spiritual happenings we've witnessed in our travels."

Marilyn likes to point out that not everything they do is about humanitarian service. "We like to travel for pleasure—from the covered bridges in Iowa to the Trans-Siberian Railroad in Russia. . . . Plus, pleasure and satisfaction are out there. You just have to search them out and go for it. And people should understand that the best things in life may also be just around the corner. You don't always have to travel. Our rich life includes birthday events, dinners with friends, and continuous communication with family and loved ones."

Clearly, Roy and Marilyn hold as a central focus service to others. Roy explains it this way: "I'm a believer that somehow you get paid back for the money you give to the needy, but more so for the deeds you do and the mental support you give to others. Hopefully, this support and these humanitarian trips will help make the world a little smaller and more friendly."

CHAPTER EIGHT

Giving of Yourself One Person at a Time

MUCH COMMUNITY SERVICE volunteer activity involves working within an organization, on the board or with committees, to support the organization itself so that its people in the field will have the resources to provide the direct service to those who need it. This means that many volunteers, while doing good organizational work, are one step removed from those who directly benefit.

Nothing wrong with that, of course, but it may not be your cup of tea. You may feel that you've spent a career in organizations of one kind or another and now you want to have hands-on involvement in whatever you choose to do. If that's the case, bless you. The opportunities are unlimited.

BIG LESSONS FROM A LITTLE QUIZ

A high school principal recently published this little quiz in the school newsletter. Before reading this chapter, try the quiz yourself.

Quiz 1

1. Name the five wealthiest people in the world.

2. Name the last five Heisman Trophy winners.

3. Name the last five winners of the Miss America contest.

4. Name ten people who have won the Nobel or Pulitzer Prize.

5. Name the last half-dozen Academy Award winners for actor and actress.

6. Name the last decade's worth of World Series winners.

How did you do? Remember that awards tarnish, achievements are forgotten, and plaques and certificates are buried with their owners. Now try Quiz 2.

But how do you decide whom to serve and what that service should be? Clearly some areas of service require specific expertise, training, or education. But there are plenty that don't. David Jordan (see his story, page 191)

Quiz 2

1. List a few teachers who aided your journey through school.

2. Name three friends who have helped you through a difficult time.

3. Name five people who have taught you something worthwhile.

4. Think of a few people who have made you feel appreciated and special.

5. Think of five people you enjoy spending time with.

6. Name half a dozen people whose stories or actions have inspired you.

The lesson is obvious. The people who make a difference in life are not necessarily the ones with the most public honors or the most money. They are the ones who care.

required no training to hold the "preemies" in the maternity ward at one of his local hospitals.

Tracy Morris, a retired administrative assistant, reads books to people who are blind or seriously visually impaired. She learned about this service from a newspaper article. "I said to myself, 'That's something I can do. I used to read to my children, and I can do this.'"

In considering service to people one at a time, I don't mean to suggest that you avoid connection with organizations. To the contrary, organizations often are the conduit to these experiences.

The Power of Listening

I once heard a man who'd been a chaplain at a home for the elderly describe the first time he entered the facility. He walked through the front door and into a large room that served as a gathering place, a lounge, and a television room. Many of the residents had assembled there to welcome him. Some sat in the room's regular chairs, others in wheelchairs; some stood slowly when he came in, leaning on canes or walkers; others stood easily without support. No one spoke, but everyone looked at him.

"They seemed to be looking at me with such great expectation," he says, "as if waiting for me to notice them or to say something. I felt suddenly that, in their silence, everybody there wanted to raise a hand, wave it at me, and shout, 'Look at me, look at me! I have a story— let me tell my story!' and I realized that my greatest job in the beginning, and perhaps throughout my tenure, would be to just listen and honor their stories."

What the chaplain understood was that, even though he was connected with an institution, his real work was to be with individual people, one at a time.

You don't have to be a chaplain or a teacher to be of personal service to people in all kinds of situations, in or out of institutions and care facilities. You just have to be a listener. Everyone has a story, whether a child or an older person or a person with a disability or serious illness; and in

> *You don't have to be a chaplain or a teacher to be of personal service to people in all kinds of situations, in or out of institutions and care facilities.*

our society, with its emphasis on achievement and celebrity, people whose lives are restricted in some way rarely get a chance to tell their stories. They struggle, but their struggles are often not recognized. They perform acts of enormous courage just in the everyday living of their lives, but their courage goes unacknowledged. It's difficult for those of us who don't face such challenges to understand what a boost it is to the spirit just to have someone show a little interest, to pay attention, to listen.

YOU CAN BE A MENTOR

Big Brothers/Big Sisters of America is the largest mentoring organization, having more than five hundred affiliates in more than five thousand communities. It matches adults with children in need of caring adults, provides training for volunteers, and supervises the relationships. You can find local organizations and get more information on their Web site: **www.bbbsa.org**. Or check your phone book's business listings for a local affiliate.

www.serviceleader.org offers information, resources, and listings for various kinds of online mentoring for volunteers.

www.savethechildren.org/mentors/ and **www .mentoring.org** have information explaining their programs. The Save the Children's 50-Plus Mentoring Program recruits, trains, and matches local adults fifty years and over with children participating in their Web of Support programs.

Some organizations focus specifically on this kind of work. Big Brothers/Big Sisters, for instance, understands that when an adult pays attention to a child who doesn't get much attention, the impact on that child's life will be felt for years.

Look for Opportunities on Your Own

My late cousin Douglas served for several years as super-intendent of education in a small county in the South. In this role, he came in contact daily with young people from all walks of life, of course, but he was particularly moved by those whose background and family situations were so debilitating that their futures were anything but promising.

One year, he met a young person who, against all odds, was struggling to do well in school and, within the constraints of her situation, was succeeding admirably. Douglas decided that she deserved more of a chance, so he and his wife established a supportive relationship in which they paid for the young person's education and expenses associated with it. She graduated from high school and attended college.

I asked Douglas why he had decided to help this per-son among all those he'd known. "She just tried so hard and wanted to succeed," he said. "She had something to give society, but without an education she'd never be able to give it. I knew that without the positive influence of an adult and without some financial support, she'd never even make it out of middle school. So we decided to help. I wish I could have helped them all, and I do hope that her achievements will inspire other kids from similar circumstances to believe they can do better. Plus,

I was hoping that other people might pick a kid and do what we did."

At his funeral a few years ago, the girl he'd supported offered a moving eulogy, and I couldn't help thinking that her very presence, her self-confidence, and her ability to address the congregation were in themselves part of his living legacy.

It's not possible for everyone to do something like this, and in many situations it wouldn't be appropriate, but there are students everywhere who need some kind of help. You could volunteer to help a teacher in the classroom by reading, helping grade papers, or, with younger children, assisting with crafts projects. In my experience, schools and teachers welcome parent and friend volunteers in the classroom. The lesson here is one of simply paying attention and being ready to respond to a need if it's possible for you to do so.

Be Willing to Share Yourself Emotionally

A few years ago, one of the social service agencies established a family support program called "Friends of New Parents," through which a woman who was about to give birth requested a "friend." The friend was a volunteer who promised to help the new mother with shopping, errands, child care, or just conversation.

Sally Pederson (my wife) signed up as a "friend" and was matched with Laura (not her real name). They became fairly close, though not what you'd call real friends. Our two families went to church together occasionally. Sally and Laura shopped and ran errands together, and Sally helped Laura get signed up for a computer training course so she could improve her economic situation.

Laura later moved and they lost touch, but Sally, who was raised in a middle-class home, said that the friendship was an eye-opener for her. She learned much about what it means to be a single mom and to struggle financially. "I benefited more than Laura did from the relationship," Sally says. "I gained a lot of knowledge, about social services, about dealing with and accessing government services, and about some of the challenges a lot of people face in our society. It made me far more sensitive to those needs."

A FEW YEARS ago, while performing an activity for the first time as an elder of my church, I was surprised to find that I was also providing a very personal service to people who are often neglected. My job was to deliver communion to "shut-ins," mostly elderly people, who no longer were able to attend church services but who desired that weekly communion continue to be a vital part of their lives.

The duty was simple enough: After the regular Sunday worship, the elders packed little boxes of communion bread and jugs of grape juice, received our list of names and addresses from the church office, and made our rounds to the individual homes.

Upon entering, we were to greet the person, share a prayer, then together eat the bread and drink the juice in the age-old ritual of communion. That was to be followed by parting pleasantries and then on to the next one.

At my first stop, however, I discovered that it was not so simple. I discovered that the act of drinking the juice and eating the bread was not the most important ritual of the day. Rather, the more important part was the human contact. These folks had waited all week for this visit, and they were ready to talk.

When I entered the first house, the woman said, "You know, you walk the way my husband used to walk, with a quick step."

Taking that as a compliment, I said, "Thank you." She continued, "My daddy wondered why I would marry a man who walked so quick."

I didn't know how to respond so said nothing while I set about preparing the communion elements. I heard all about her late husband and his job, his World War II experiences, and the early years of their marriage. Suddenly I understood that the real communion was between us, the two of us plus the memories of other people in her life. I confess I never felt a deeper sense of communion than in those visits.

JOANN ZIMMERMAN SAW a need, created her own opportunity, and then was courageous enough to share herself emotionally. The results have been extraordinary.

JoAnn was thirty-nine years old and had worked in financial institutions all her life. One morning she woke up thinking, "If I could do anything I wanted with the rest of my life, what would it be?" She felt anyone could do what she did just as well as she did it, and she wanted to feel her innate gifts were being put to use in the world. The question would not go away.

After much quiet reflection, she realized she had two strong gifts: one was a love for children, and the second was compassion. "Put those together, quit your job, and become a bear," she told herself, "then you can be a caring presence in the community."

Her idea was simple: Dress up like a big lovable bear and go to schools and teach children to be more caring and sensitive. She chose a panda because this type is nonfrightening, playful, and friendly, and she named the bear Amanda, which means "worthy of love or needing to be loved."

She tried to work within the structure of the savings and loan where she was employed and rewrote her job description to be a caring bear that would be the company's quiet but loving messenger of compassion to children.

Her company thought it was a great plan to be in the community, but their idea was to use the program to teach children the difference between banks and savings and loans. Another thing: Rather than a bear, the S&L people wanted her to dress up like a dollar bill with legs.

She rejected both of these ideas and worked until she saved up the $1,200 it would cost to create a panda costume. That was in 1980. She started visiting schools as Amanda the Panda, according to her plan, and soon got a call from a hospice about a young boy with an inoperable brain tumor. They asked whether she would visit him. This visit changed her profoundly, and she had a new calling.

Then children began writing to her or telling her of other seriously ill or dying children. She began visiting children in their homes throughout her state, accompanying them back to school after chemotherapy and teaching the other kids how to be sensitive to the changes in their friends.

In 1984 she created Camp-A-Panda to give children living with cancer a week-long thrill of summer camp, allowing them to be children first and cancer patients second. During the time JoAnn was raising funds for the summer camp, she created Camp Amanda, a weekend camp for children who were grieving a death in their family. She later added a similar camp for adults and is now working with other organizations to start camps in several states.

JoAnn has never charged a penny for her services. She founded Amanda Cares, Inc., to be a nonprofit organization with a staff of volunteers. For twenty-two years, she has helped scores of children leave this world surrounded by love and compassion, and she has taught scores more children (and their parents) how to pass on that sensitivity and cope with their grief at losing friends and family.

For more information, see the Web site at www. Amandathepanda.org.

SERVING PEOPLE ONE at a time often requires a lot of spiritual stamina, as indeed it does for JoAnn Zimmerman and her volunteer pandas, and it could be that you'd prefer an organizational setting, as described in the previous chapter. But as you have read, the potential for personal and spiritual growth through making yourself available emotionally to another person is enormous.

> *The potential for personal and spiritual growth through making yourself available emotionally to another person is enormous.*

Questions to Ask Yourself

In making a decision to pursue opportunities for this kind of service, however, you should ask some honest questions of yourself:

1. What are my real motives? Do I want to engage actively over a period of time in helping, or is this just an impulse of sympathy that may be short-lived? (There's nothing wrong with the sympathetic impulse, but perhaps another way to respond would be more realistic for your situation or inclinations.)

2. Do I really want to make this kind of commitment to another person, realizing that it will require not only emotional strength but also the time to be appropriately responsive?

3. Do I have the strength or courage simply to be exposed to people with these kinds of needs and challenges? (It's no disgrace to devote your service efforts in a more detached or abstract way through an organization or simply through donations.)

4. How will my spouse or life partner feel about this and about the time it may require? Is there a way for both of us to be involved, and would that be desirable?

If you can answer these questions to your satisfaction, you will be ready to start on this great adventure, a journey of hope and healing to other people, and a source of satisfaction and spiritual growth in your retirement life.

VIRGINIA'S STORY

Put Your Experience and Wisdom to Work in the World

One thing that seems to come with maturity is a greater ability to listen, to be present, and to bring your experience and wisdom to bear in the world. Certainly, retirement provides the time to nurture those qualities, but each of us has to make the opportunity. Virginia Traxler's opportunity presented itself in the birth of a child.

Virginia's life changed forever when, within a period of two months, she witnessed two of her grandchildren being born while she was also spending time with her dying father. For Virginia, these experiences put her in the presence of the Divine.

"There is an intensity of feeling and a presence of divinity when human beings enter and leave life on Earth," she says. "Being present to people in that process feels like life in its clearest moment, its most basic essence."

Virginia spent many years as a teacher, counselor, and therapist. A few years ago, when she had retired from those pursuits, her stepdaughter, Julia, invited her to be present at the birth of her first child. Virginia was thrilled. "I had never been present for a birth of any child other than my own," she says. "Watching that baby come into the world moved the earth under my feet, and I was profoundly changed."

Two months later, she was present when her daughter-in-law Courtney gave birth. What Virginia noticed at that time is that she seemed imbued with a sense of exactly what to do, of how to be with Courtney in ways that were comforting to her.

"It felt familiar, as if I had done it before," she explains. "I was propelled into the birthing world. The word *doula* became part of my vocabulary, and my education began."

A *doula* is a woman who supports a birthing woman physically, emotionally, and spiritually before and during labor. Virginia felt called to be a doula and studied it passionately. She spent time at The Farm in Tennessee, learning from The Farm midwives, a group that has done more home births than any other people in the country. Virginia learned about prenatal care, how to use herbs and tinctures, the physiology of labor and birth, and, most important, trusting a woman's body.

"I felt like I was in the midst of the wisdom of the grandmothers," she says.

"Giving birth is an act of courage. It requires faith and trust, both in the process of birth as well as in a woman's body. A doula brings that faith and trust to the birthing place."

Virginia considers her calling as a doula to have been one of the great blessings of her life, even though she recognizes the blessings of having worked with and helped many schoolchildren and others in trouble over the years.

"There are many times in our lives when we have the opportunity to be present with the Divine," she says, "but we must step up and be in them, be willing to stand in the presence of divinity even when we tremble with fear.

"As a doula, I can help a woman and her partner be present to the miracle. When I am with a woman as she labors, I witness her pain, her courage, her triumph. Having been witnessed, it is like a legal document; it becomes real."

As with many first experiences, Virginia will never forget her first as a doula. "It was with Barbara, a single woman who knew almost nothing about birth but knew she wanted a companion. When her water broke, I met her at the hospital. We walked the halls for an hour or so, and then came the edict from on high: The doctor said to start pitocin. Pitocin is a drug that stimulates the uterus and starts contractions or increases their strength. The doctor did not come to talk to her about the procedure, what her options were, or why it was necessary.

"The nurse came and took Barbara out of the halls, put her in bed, and started an IV. Contractions began and got harder and harder for her to handle. She could have nothing to eat or drink but ice chips. I massaged her, I talked to her, I encouraged her, and at the end I crawled into bed with her and held her.

"She gave birth to her baby girl without ever having asked for drugs even though she had said all along that she wanted them. She was proud beyond measure.

"And so it began. I learned something new with each birth."

One of the things Virginia had to learn was patience. She has spent a lot of time waiting. "Beginning two weeks before the due date, everything in a doula's life is second to the coming labor. Am I planning a dinner party? I know I may not be there. Have I promised to take my grandchildren to the zoo? I may not be available. The church committee I chair is meeting? I may not be in attendance. Am I planning to go out to my favorite restaurant with my husband to celebrate our anniversary? He may eat alone. I can't commit. I may not be there.

"It is three in the morning. Labor begins. I am exhausted. But I must be there. So whenever nature decides the time is now, no matter what is going on in my own life, as a doula, I go to the woman in labor, to hold her hand, rub her back, walk with her, sit with her, tell her how brave she is, and wait with her, patiently wait. Morning may turn into night and night to morning, while, one contraction at a time, birth unfolds.

"What is hard to express in a way that has meaning is the suspension of time, the tediousness of hours and hours of waiting, waiting with someone who is in pain. Being with someone in pain requires acceptance, a willingness to *not* try to fix it but to just be fully present in body, mind, and spirit. My muscles often ache from being in the same position for long periods of time. If I find one thing that works—back pressure, applied heat, stroking—I may do it for hours."

Virginia's passion for her calling extends to a sense of greater purpose for women. "If we want women to participate in bringing the feminine to the world, bringing balance to our war-torn Earth, being full participants in the effort to save the environment, find cures for disease and famine, and help heal all that plagues the Earth, then women must know and live into their feminine energy and power. Giving birth is one of the most transforming and powerful experiences a woman can ever have."

Does Virginia feel that she is helping save the world, one woman at a time? "Absolutely," she says. But her focus is not on herself; it's on the women.

"I've learned so much. I learned to read fear in a woman's eyes. I learned the calming power of touch. I learned the importance of assuring a woman that she is safe. I learned the difference it makes whether a woman chooses a doctor or a midwife. I learned that for a woman to choose how she gives birth is a political act. I learned that even though I carry a bag with me with many things to help a woman in labor, my most valuable tools are my hands, my eyes, and my voice. I learned to watch for clues in partnerships and to help a woman's partner be with her in ways that comforted."

Virginia refuses to label her calling as a profession. "It is important to recognize and understand that doulaing as a business or profession is almost a contradiction, because it can really never be anything but a gift. There are some human experiences on which a price cannot be placed.

"What would I pay to have someone sitting at my bedside holding my hand when it is my time to die? What is it worth to know that my children are in loving and nurturing hands when they cannot be with me? What a doula gives at birth is just as priceless. She chooses to give it. She serves with love."

PART FOUR

Time for the World Around You

MOST OF US have spent our work lives in the midst of that great dualism: We were at home or at work, at home or at work, except for the all-too-short weekends and those rare times we were able to get away for a vacation. And sometimes those vacations were on such a tight schedule and were filled with such activity that when we returned, we felt we had to rest up for a day or so before we could go back to work.

We told ourselves that this was not the way vacations were supposed to be, that our leisure time should provide something beyond another series of obligatory places to be and things to see, all on a tight schedule. At those times, we probably looked forward to retirement and more time to do the things we wanted to do.

Not everyone vacationed in this way, of course, and you may have been (or may be) one of those sensible people who really knew (knows) how to take time off and how to spend a truly relaxing vacation. Even so, chances are that you, too, were recharging the batteries so that you could return to work ready to hit it hard again, full speed ahead.

A retirement life in endless perpetuation of the same old activities can become a life with steadily decreasing opportunities for meaning and growth.

For most people, vacations have not been times in which they concentrated on learning or on growing personally. When they retire, they often continue the pattern of leisure activity they've become accustomed to: golf, tennis, fishing, bowling, and so on. There's nothing wrong with those interests, but a retirement life in endless perpetuation of the same old activities can become a life with steadily decreasing opportunities for meaning and growth.

This section continues its offerings of ideas and inspiration on the path of personal growth by examining two areas that are not unique but that may be approached in uniquely spiritual ways: wilderness experiences and gardening.

DAVID'S STORY
From Hobby to Passion

When we think of "hobby," we often have the image of an activity that may engage us as a way to pass the time and "do something interesting," but we rarely think of it as a source of passion. Yet a hobby can indeed become a passion, especially when two or more interests converge in a way that is not predictable or expected. Take David Jordan's hobby, for instance.

David has been a U.S. naval officer, a magazine editor, a professional photographer, and a designer and master woodworker. Throughout his professional life, he maintained a strong interest in the environment and the natural world, and now in retirement, he travels thousands of miles to photograph insects in the rain forest.

Like a lot of people who retire, David did not want to let his professional skills fade away, especially photography, which requires practice and a continuing awareness of technological advances and innovations. On the other hand, he was no longer interested in the kinds of photography he'd done as a professional.

His interest in the natural sciences led him to take up insect photography a few years before his retirement. At first, he simply walked in his wife's flower garden, looking and shooting. "As I progressed, however," he says, "I quickly got beyond 'Oh, there's a pretty one' into a fascination with the enormous profusion of insect life and the weird life cycles of these wonderful creatures. Over the years, I've become a fair to middlin' entomologist."

Shortly after his retirement, David discovered an opportunity to put his skills together with his concern for the Earth. He learned about Earthwatch, an international organization that sponsors the field research of a wide variety of scientists. The organization recruits volunteers from all over the world and from all walks of life for these expeditions to do the essential grunt work that is the foundation of all field research.

"I was delighted to find that several of the trips involved studies in tropical forests in South and Central America and concerned insects in some way," David says. As a volunteer, he was required to pay a fee to Earthwatch, which helps with the cost of the particular expedition and also covers some of the organizational overhead. Each volunteer is also responsible for the round-trip travel costs to the study site.

David signed up first for a study entitled "Peruvian Katydids" and soon was on his way to Iquitos, Peru.

"I know this sounds pretty esoteric," David says, "but that's the nature of scientific research, and what I've learned about research over the years is that you never know what the eventual impact of a study might be. Katydids, as it happens, are so numerous in tropical forests that they constitute the main base of the food chain. It is very important to study them."

As with most Earthwatch expeditions, a dozen or so volunteers were in David's group. Their leader was David Nickle, an entomologist from the Smithsonian, who was conducting a census of katydid species.

"We spent the next two weeks in three lodges that ranged along the Amazon downriver from Iquitos. The living conditions were comfortable enough, on a summer camp level, and the companionship of the other volunteers was delightful. Their ages varied from the early twenties to a couple of us retired types. I think I was the old guy in the group, as I was on the five Earthwatch trips I've done so far."

The work itself involved catching katydids and preparing the collected specimens for transport back to the Smithsonian. "As with so many basic facts about the tropics," David explains, "there is very little notion of how many species of katydids exist. I began to get my first insight into the importance of quantification in this kind of study.

"We got up before dawn each morning and made our way into the forest to a tree that had been selected the day before. We spread sheets of plastic all around the base of the tree, then Dave Nickle sent a plume of short-lived insecticide up the tree, using a noisy blower we dubbed the Death Star. Soon, insects rained down onto the plastic, to be collected and roughly sorted by us volunteers."

It was a bit of a shock to David that insecticide was used to collect the specimens. "At first, this didn't seem consonant with what I thought of as saving the Earth, but then I came to realize that this was the only way to collect the specimens, and I was satisfied that the chemical used was short-lived and would do no residual damage. Also I understood that the people involved were just as concerned for the Earth as I was."

After breakfast, the group returned to the tree to gather any stragglers and to clean up their plastic sheets. The rest of the day was spent preparing specimens, with some time set aside for David to photograph them.

There was also time for him to photograph other insects and to make private expeditions into the forest. Sometimes it was these walks that gave David a deeper sense of connection with the forest and made him understand even more intensely just why he had taken on this work.

"I had visited tropical forests before but never had the chance to experience one so intimately. I found that I could walk just a few feet into the edge of the forest, stand quietly for a few moments, and then see some wonderment of nature: a procession of leaf-cutter ants, each bearing a fragment of leaf back to feed the underground fungus garden in their nest, or a multicolored slime mold creeping across a log like something from a science fiction movie. And of course the insects were there by the thousands, in all shapes and sizes, some so bizarre as to almost defy belief.

"It makes me sad to realize that at the rate the tropical forests are being destroyed, they may disappear within the next fifty years. And they are home to 95 percent of the species on Earth."

David's five Earthwatch expeditions have each been a different study, but all contributing to the mosaic of basic research trying to piece together an understanding of the tropical forests. For David, this volunteer work is not a matter of having fun, though he finds plenty of enjoyment and fellowship in them. But there are also poisonous snakes, stinging insects, and plain hard work.

"Sometimes it's exhausting, like the days I spent measuring and tagging acacia trees in Mexico in hundred-degree heat and 100 percent humidity, being stung every few minutes by the ants protecting the trees.

"And sometimes the task gives the volunteers the giggles, like last summer when we found ourselves collecting caterpillar poop from plastic traps in the forest, drying it and weighing it.

"But more often than not the work is simply fascinating: days spent in the forest searching for caterpillars, or capturing and tagging euglossine bees that pollinate orchids—all in the company of an international group of volunteers and a scientist willing to share his encyclopedic knowledge of the forest."

Then there may be the rare, very rare, opportunity to participate in something no one else on Earth has ever seen. Last year, David was the first person to photograph a little jumping spider eating a protein capsule from the leaf of an acacia tree, a never-before-recorded phenomenon.

This is the entomologist's equivalent of discovering another planet.

For most of us, it may seem extraordinarily strange to spend precious time and money to brave the rigors of the tropical forest to photograph spiders, or collect katydids, or weigh caterpillar poop, but for someone with David's reverence for the Earth, this is a passion.

He puts it this way: "The research of the Earthwatch teams is helping salvage the secrets of the forest and, perhaps, find the incentives for humanity to save this irreplaceable resource. I'm grateful to be a small part of it."

CHAPTER NINE

Finding the Spirit in Nature's Wild Places

In wildness is the preservation of the world.
—Henry David Thoreau

"COMMUNING WITH NATURE" is something we tend to think of as the stuff only of poets and philosophers, but the truth is that a regular connection with the natural world can imbue all of us with a little poetry and philosophy. The wilderness can be a window into a greater understanding of life itself. It's no accident that many of the great thinkers, leaders, and philosophers, from Jesus to Buddha and from Thoreau to Teddy Roosevelt, found not only inspiration but also answers to life's great questions "in the wilderness."

There is still much opportunity for a wilderness experience and for the spiritual growth it can provide.

Although you can explore wilderness areas in much the same way as our early settlers did, you need not brave the beasts, snakes, and mosquitoes to have a true experience of being in the wild. You need not take an African safari or travel to a tropical rain forest as David Jordan does. You don't even need to be in a particularly large or remote area.

> *The wilderness can be a window into a greater understanding of life itself.*

The objective of an experience in the wild is not so much about isolation or the lack of civilization or the flora and fauna as it is about letting yourself be fully present in the natural world, letting all your senses fill with the sights, sounds, smells, and feel of an environment entirely different from where you have spent your daily life.

If you have no experience outside a city or town, other than an occasional visit to a park, and if you want a relatively easy way to explore nature, start with a national forest. One of America's treasures is our system of national parks and national forests. You undoubtedly know about the parks and perhaps have visited some of them. Less known are the national forests. This is an incredible system of 155 forests and 20 grasslands located in almost every part of the country. These lands are generally open to the public, though there are restrictions on camping and particularly on campfires. Otherwise, you are free to explore them, some of which contain huge areas of wilderness and others that are smaller but still have zones of what might be called "microwilderness." Some require that you stay on marked trails, others that you register at a ranger station, and so on. Some are more developed and offer welcome centers, museums, and nature tours. Whatever your willingness or physical ability, you can have a wilderness experience in a national forest even if you are only yards from a marked trail.

The National Forest Service's Web site, **www.fs.fed.us**, tells you about the Forest Service, has links to the individual national forests Web sites, and gives information on recreation, heritage, and wilderness programs. The National Parks Service also has a Web site: **www.nps.gov/parks.html**. You can search for parks by recreational interest, location, or key words. The pages at the individual parks list what each park offers, its history, fees and restrictions, and other basic information. It also contains maps and explains the park system, including ways to volunteer.

My nephew John is a partially retired building contractor in Georgia. He recently decided to walk the Appalachian Trail all the way to Maine. It will be a rough and ready trip, camping out in all kinds of weather and walking for many miles every day. I asked why he wanted to do it.

"I've always liked being in the forest, and I've always wanted to live in the wilderness for more than a few days

ANOTHER HELPFUL WEB SITE

www.Gorp.com bills itself as "Your Guide to Outdoor Recreation and Active Travel." It has information on all kinds of travel locations and adventures all over the world, complete with staff rankings in a multitude of categories. Check out its Top 10 National Forests and other national forest information at wwwgorp.com /gorp/resource/topten/forests.htm. The site (GORP stands for Great Outdoor Recreation Pages) was started in 1995 and is run by a couple of outdoor enthusiasts who strive to provide complete information for people wanting to explore their outdoor environment, from the far-flung wilderness to their backyard. You can search by destination, activities, and interests. They also offer books, gear, and free GORP memberships for discussions, events, and ratings of more than 1,400 parks.

at a time," he says. "I now have a few months with nothing scheduled, so this seemed like a rare opportunity to walk some of the same mountain trails our ancestors walked when they came South to settle."

His wife supports this adventure, but she'll remain at home during the four months or so that he'll be gone. Does she mind? "Not at all. This is one of those life experiences not many people have had. I think it will do a lot for John's spirit and his creativity."

In listening to John, I discovered that there is now a regular program for those who want to walk the Appalachian Trail, or even just part of it.

The Appalachian Trail has more than 500 access points along its 2,167 miles. People hike it by day, weekend, and other short periods. Through-hikers hike the entire length of the trail in a season. Most hikers do not use guides, but they are available along some sections.

Numerous sources for information about the trail are available on the Internet:

www.appalachiantrail.org/hike. This site of the thirty-one-member conference of clubs and organizations that maintain and promote the Appalachian Trail offers many resources for experiencing the trail. It lists the member groups that offer guided tours and events, or you can contact the AT conference for a packet of information on how to hike the trail: Appalachian Trail Conference, 799 Washington St., PO Box 807, Harpers Ferry, WV 25425-0807; (304)535-6331; fax: (304) 535-2667.

www.nps.gov/appa is the National Park Service's description of features of the trail.

www.Trailplace.com. Run by the Center for Appalachian Trail Studies, this site gives a wealth of information, maps, chat rooms, and references for hiking the trail, including nature and wildlife along the trail.

The Water View of Wilderness

An experience in the wild does not have to be about trekking through the forest, however. There is also much beautiful country to be experienced from a boat. You can take whitewater rafting trips on wild rivers, of course— an adventure in the wild, to be sure—but I prefer float trips on meandering streams through forest lands. Quiet, easy-moving water has a way of creating a serene and meditative atmosphere that enriches your already intensely attuned senses.

As you go softly with the current, you are frequently rewarded by the sight of various kinds of wildlife that, because they don't expect a predator from the water, often won't even notice you in a boat. It's an experience I've had hundreds of times in the relatively unforested state of Iowa and along the Sewanee River, deep in the marshy woodlands south of the famous Okefenokee Swamp.

Even a public lake in a park provides an entire ecosystem to observe. One hour in a boat or on the bank, just watching twenty feet of shoreline, you can find all the drama of life. There is something about sharing space with the natural inhabitants of a wild place, even if only for moments, that transports me to another level of awareness about all the life on this Earth and what a gift it is to all of us.

Finding a Hobby in the Wild

Donald Mitchell, a soon-to-be-retired employee of the Small Business Administration, feels this same deep sense of connection with the wilderness as he counts butterflies.

"When I returned to my native state of California after an absence of twenty-seven years," he says, "I wanted to get in touch with the wilderness I remembered from my boyhood. I found that much of it remained, though in somewhat modified states.

"Because I had a friend who was interested in insects, I decided that I, too, would become interested. While driving in the desert, I began to stop, walk in the wilderness, and look at plants and bugs.

"Then I joined a bug organization, the Xerces Society. A group of Xerces officers then decided to begin a new organization called the North American Butterfly Association, so I joined that, too, and before long went to the national convention. In the past fourteen years, I've joined other insect and bug groups. Among ourselves we call them 'invertebrates.'

"The butterfly group now counts local butterflies in predetermined spots all over the nation every year and publishes the results. I've been involved with that for

HOW TO FIND YOUR OWN CONNECTION
WITH THE NATURAL WORLD

A group of Web sites fall under **www.familyofnature .com**. It's sponsored by Family of Nature, Inc., and has wonderful resources for a host of wildlife. There's a free newsletter, chat rooms, a photo gallery, The Nature Store, and sections for getting involved with wildlife, gardening, and conservation. At the bottom of the Free Newsletter page are links to sites about butterflies, ornithology, wildlife gardening, dragonflies, hummingbirds, and frogs and toads. The individual sites have all kinds of information about the subject, plus listings of zoos, gardens, and museums that feature each species.

For example, **www.butterflywebsite.com** has opportunities for volunteering, quizzes and games involving

several years. I speak to school groups and other nature organizations and show slides."

I asked Don why a guy would get involved in such an esoteric activity. I said I understand and accept the desire to preserve butterflies and that the count is an important indicator of environmental impact. But, while I didn't want to push him beyond his comfort level in talking about his inner life, I wondered whether there was a more

butterfly facts, a live newsfeed on a recent event about butterflies, links to societies, and listings of nature field trips and public butterfly gardens all over the world.

For insect zoos, gardens, and museums, look at the Entomological Society of America's Web site, **www.entsoc.org.** Under Education and Information are resources, including projects with schools and frequently asked questions. The listing of public places in North America is under the Links of Entomological Interest in that section.

For opportunities to work or experience butterflies, insects, and other wildlife closer to home, check with your county extension office about classes, programs, and locations. This is one of the great unknown and underappreciated sources of information and activity.

deeply personal aspect he could offer for the readers of this book. His answer provides a compellingly spiritual reason for this way of experiencing the wildness.

"My entire interest in this was not to see how butterflies fit into the environment," he says. "It was rather to see how *I* fit into the environment. This probably came to me in the most intense way when I was touring a remote part of the Amazon River and surrounding jungle in Peru.

Lots of bugs, lots of trees, lots of birds, lots of fish, and just a very few people. It looked like it was meant to all get along together, to work together like parts of an engine. But in many places on Earth the engine is broken. Hiking in nature with the specific purpose of looking for butterflies to see what they are doing—I'm more of a behaviorist than taxonomist—gives me focus of the larger picture: the relationships of all of the living things here. And [to realize that] everything here is living in the larger sense of eternal time, even the sand and the rocks."

Don's experience and testimony are not unusual among people who have chosen to focus their wilderness explorations on a particular interest, such as wildflowers or trees or fish or reptiles or birds, all of which provide a wide variety of ways and places to be in the wild.

Defining Wilderness

In discussing the potential for finding meaning and for nurturing your inner life through experiences in the natural world, I have not suggested that there is only one way to be "in the wild." Some enthusiasts would insist on defining that activity as being in a remote wilderness, away from all civilization, but that response would be missing the larger point.

You can be in nature in a national park or in a city park, in small places such as a pocket park in a city, on the bank of a lake, on a bike trail along an urban river, or in your car on a rural back road. The only requirement is that you be willing to embrace fully the nature all around you, to listen, to see, and to think reflectively and meditatively about how, in Don Mitchell's words, "it was all meant to work together" and about how "everything here is living in the larger sense of eternal time."

Which, of course, includes you.

JEANNE'S STORY

A Life of Spirituality Can Be an Active Life

Jeanne Cahill asks, rhetorically, "How can gardening not be spiritual?" then adds, "Sometimes I feel the very form of a tree is more inspirational that most sermons I've heard."

She also shares a favorite quote: "Planting a tree is the most optimistic thing you can ever do." And Jeanne has planted trees in every home she and her husband, Al, have owned. "I did it for the benefit of others who would be there in years to come. Now I like to drive by those places to see how the landscape has matured."

Her commitment to gardening is deeply spiritual. "I'd rather hold a water hose than turn on a sprinkler because there is something about being the intermediary of the life-giving water that is satisfying. So is saving kitchen scraps for compost and seeing it mix into clay to restore its ability to produce life. I feel as if I'm participating in Earth's rhythms.

"And planting a tree is my way of leaving a sermon whether anyone ever realizes it or not. Daddy always taught us that we should leave the world a better place; planting trees is one of the ways I try to do that."

Jeanne and Al have lived active lives and have been involved in a variety of business enterprises. Most recently, Jeanne owned and managed a very successful exercise equipment company. When one of her friends began talking about retirement several years ago, it caused her to think about her own plans. "There was no real planning," she says, "but rather a period of introspection: What did I want to do that work had prevented? Where did I want to live? What activities would I share with Al? What was my passion? Did I want to go back to college? I made a list then added to it and subtracted from it from time to time. I knew that lifelong learning was important to me, but I wasn't sure what I wanted to learn. Instead of specifics, I listened, watched, read, learned what others were doing—or not doing— and began to have ideas.

"This informal planning I did was right for me because I had so many areas of interest that it was a matter of choosing between the good and the good. Spiritual growth was not a specific goal, but I knew I wanted to do things to benefit others while giving me a sense of purpose. And I wanted time for contemplation."

Jeanne defines *spiritual* as "those acts which help refine one's thoughts and character as they relate to humanity and nature; a way of living which enhances the soul, which harms no one, and which leaves the world a better place because you passed by."

Her own active spirituality divides itself into two rather specific areas: quiet pursuits that focus on feeding her own spirit and those activities that involve interactions with others.

In addition to gardening, Jeanne has recently begun to work in clay as another way to be in touch with nature. "My experience with pottery is unexpectedly spiritual for me. The clay is so elemental—weren't we supposedly formed from it?—and there is a special feeling in just handling the substance and seeing it take form. All my pieces so far have had a nature connection—impressions of leaves, berries, flowers, and some slithery snakes. The glazes have been earth tones. I find also that I am more prone to making vessels such as bowls, plates, and vases which are useful and nice to hold, ready to receive something so it becomes an interactive 'thing' with the person who receives it. I give away everything I make, except the flawed ones."

Jeanne says that, even though it has been five years, the "new" hasn't worn off retirement. "I think the secret is diversity," she says. "Al and I have things to do as a couple, yet each of us has individual interests of our own. We both remain open to opportunities."

In turning much of her active spirituality toward others, Jeanne focuses on rituals with family and friends, "simple things like inviting people in for dessert and coffee or a light supper." And she believes in being a good friend, in working to be a good person who cares about others and practices random acts of kindness, particularly with relatives.

Several times during the year, she and her sister Lynda visit their ninety-year-old mother and work in her garden. "Lynda and I will set aside everything we have to do and just make the trip. We always love seeing Mother and working in her garden, although she would probably prefer that we just sit and visit with her and forget the garden. We ease the problem by positioning her near our work site with a good CD playing and a glass of wine in her hands. She keeps us supplied with her good iced tea and pecan pie, and if it were not for profuse sweating, our bodies would probably go into sugar shock."

Jeanne has not gone back to college but is "self-educating through participation in a book club, Joseph Campbell Mythological Roundtable, and Great Decisions, a national organization under the auspices of the state department."

In addition, she is still involved in many political and civic activities, including an appointment by the governor to serve on a student finance commission. She regularly writes letters to the editor of the local paper, attends government council and commission meetings, and goes to art openings and most of the live entertainment in the area.

"I know this sounds like a lot of activity," she says, "but I am never agitated about it, never feel rushed or stressed, and consider all of it part of my personal growth. I also know that it helps give my life meaning."

There's one other thing that Jeanne emphasizes: living a healthy and balanced life physically. "A lot of people don't seem to realize that it is easier to nourish their spirits and to focus on spiritual growth if they keep their bodies healthy. I work out in my exercise room and follow good nutritional habits because I feel it is incumbent upon each of us to stay as healthy as circumstances and effort will permit. In addition, I recycle, avoid conspicuous consumption, and try to live in harmony with humankind and with nature."

> *"A lot of people don't seem to realize that it is easier to nourish their spirits and to focus on spiritual growth if they keep their bodies healthy."*

Jeanne was born near a small town in Georgia, one of eight children, in what today we would call meager circumstances but what in those days was typical of the rural South. She treasures the lessons of her childhood.

"Although there was no cash, food was plentiful. Daddy kept patching up the old car, we girls wore flour sack dresses, and Mother took eggs, chickens, and vegetables to the country store in exchange for staples. The amazing thing is I never felt poor and never heard my parents discuss a shortage of money.

"And there was never the slightest doubt in my mind that we children were the most important thing in the world to our parents. I especially thank my late father for teaching me to be a good steward in the world and my mother for instilling a positive attitude in all things and a recognition of the blessings of my life. Amen!"

Amen indeed.

CHAPTER TEN

Connecting with Nature One Plant at a Time

THE IMAGE OF the old retiree puttering around in the garden, yelling at the dogs and neighborhood kids when they run across the manicured lawn or through the flowers, is a staple of television sitcoms and newspaper comic strips. This characterization, like most overblown stereotypes, demeans retired people as dull and irascible; not only that, it ridicules gardening as something the old folks do to keep them busy until the day they fall over and pass on to that great rose bed in the sky.

Yet working the soil and planting seeds is a primal activity that has engaged human beings since they first discovered they did not have to move from place to place, hunting and gathering food, but could make the land produce. Who knows how that understanding first entered the human consciousness, but it did, and it is still true that a need for connection with the land is deeply embedded within us. Though most of us live in urban and suburban settings, that need manages to find expression in everything from pocket gardens to houseplants.

> The truth is that there is something profoundly spiritual about working with plants.

The truth is that there is something profoundly spiritual about working with plants, and if you can't seek nature in the wilderness, or choose not to, you can still experience the vast mysteries of the natural world and gain a sense of wonder and gratitude in the simple act of gardening. In many ways, this may be the most convenient and least expensive way to enrich a retirement of personal growth.

Plants and Memory

I have been a gardener for many years, growing both flowers and vegetables. It connects me with the Earth in a way I was connected as a child in the South, and it gives me a chance to participate in the mystery of creation. Spare me the scientific explanations of how a tiny tomato seed can produce a summer's worth of fruit; regardless of how we explain the process, it still seems a miracle to me.

216

Every year I grow a tomato that has been in my family for generations. I'm told that this variety was in existence at the time of Abraham Lincoln. I always make sure to harvest at least two or three large, meaty tomatoes just for the seeds, then carefully dry the seeds and put them in the freezer to plant the next year. The tomatoes are large, pink, and rough-looking, but they are delicious; when I harvest the first one each year, I think of that act as a memorial to my late cousin, who handed down the seeds to me as they had been handed down to him.

I have grown okra and collard greens purely as a reminder to myself and other members of the family of the kind of food the family lived on for generations. And when any member of the family is within earshot and will sit still long enough to listen, I tell the ancient okra story. Okra, as I hope you know, is slimy when boiled or steamed or baked. It's what gives gumbo its wonderful texture. Well, the story is that one time a southern farm wife threw a leftover bowl of okra to the dogs. As farm dogs will do, they raced one another to the food. The dog who got there first began to growl and bite the other dogs because the okra went down so slick he thought they beat him to it.

My sons groan when I start to tell this one, but I always admonish them: "Someday I'll be gone and one of you will have the responsibility of telling the story. So listen."

There are two large pots of azaleas that I nurture through the winter in my little greenhouse and then through the summer in a shady spot on the patio. When November comes, they begin to bloom, and by Thanksgiving and Christmas they are spectacular, at least three feet across and full of blossoms. I place them among some four-foot-high Norfolk pines that I keep in the house year-round.

Here's the story of those plants: Eleven years ago, the centerpieces at my retirement dinner were made up of tiny Norfolk pines and one-blossom azaleas. I brought home some of the centerpieces, potted the plants, and over the years have nurtured and repotted them as they've grown and flourished. Every year when the azaleas bloom, I imagine they are rejoicing that I took early retirement and that I'm still around.

Cocreating Life in the Garden

Just as Marti Sivi feels the presence of God when she's with the women in her prison theater group and Virginia Traxler witnesses a Divine act in the birth of a baby, so, too, does Jeanne Cahill think of a seed as containing a spark of the Sacred (see her story, page 208).

She told me of a neighbor and friend who considers gardening a personal partnership with God. The friend experiments with seeds and plants, spending winter hours in his small, homemade greenhouse and summer hours in the garden. "He always overplants," Jeanne says. "That way, he has enough produce to keep all his friends and neighbors supplied throughout the summer. And in early spring, he gives everyone he knows a small geranium plant for their garden or windowbox. It's his way of staying in touch with an old way of doing things, of sharing in the community, of simply being a good neighbor."

I have a friend who is in quest of the perfect vegetables. Every year he tries new varieties as well as heirloom seeds of varieties a hundred years old. He keeps meticulous records, invites friends for taste testing, and rates the results on his own scorekeeping system. That may seem extreme, but that's the kind of passion that gardening can inspire.

Another of Jeanne Cahill's friends plants a tree every year, either on his own property or in cooperation with neighbors or a civic project. He shares Jeanne's attitude that planting a tree is the single most optimistic thing a person can do. He says, "I know I'll never live to enjoy the shade of some of these trees, but somebody will. It gives me pleasure to think about it."

If You Don't Have Space for a Garden

If you have a window, shady or sunny, you can have a garden. It may contain only one plant, but it will be a garden nevertheless, and if that's the only way you have to

HEIRLOOM SEEDS

Planting heirloom seeds is almost like being directly in touch with our ancestors. These seeds are from the original stock. They've never been hybridized, so in planting them you are planting direct descendents of seeds that were part of our country's history.

Sources for heirloom seeds include the following:

Heirloom Seeds, a small family-run seed house in Pennsylvania, sells non-hybrid seeds for hundreds of varieties of flowers, vegetables, and herbs. It has an online catalog you can download, or request a printed version from its mailing address: PO Box 245, West Elizabeth, PA 15088-0245; **www.heirloomseeds.com**.

Baker Creek Heirloom Seeds also offers non-hybrid seeds for hundreds of American and European heir-

grow something, that will be enough. That one plant can still provide a sense of oneness with nature and a sense that you are participating directly in the great mystery of life. A windowsill full of African violets can be enough, or with a little more ambition but very little effort, you can have a small herb garden in pots; you can even create your own miniature desert or tropical jungle in a terrar-

loom vegetables and flowers. For a free catalog, contact this source at 2278 Baker Creek Road, Mansfield, MO 65704; **www.rareseeds.com.**

Underwood Gardens bills itself as "Grandma's Garden" and specializes in "hard-to-find, open-pollinated and heirloom seeds" for flowers and vegetables. It also has products and books on organic and safe gardening practices. Contact Underwood Gardens at 1414 Zimmerman Road, Woodstock, IL 60098; **www.underwoodgardens.com.**

Another highly recommended and reliable source is *Seed Savers Exchange*, 3076 North Winn Road, Decorah, IA 52101; **www.seedsavers.org.**

ium. And just as some people love to sit close to an aquarium and gaze at the fish, you can almost project yourself into the terrarium and become a wanderer in the desert or jungle. I've heard it described as a "Zen experience."

The point is not in how many plants you have or in their variety; it's not how big your garden is or even how big your plant may grow. The point is how you feel about all this, how you engage it, how you are able to be reflective and meditative as you water or prune or feed the plants, as you work the soil, or as you just sit and take in the beauty.

How to Get Started

You may think you just don't have a "green thumb." I've heard people say things like, "Plants don't like me. They die in my house." I suspect that it's the people who don't like the plants because there are vast sources of information and advice about growing any plant imaginable. There's little reason to fail at it.

One simple and inexpensive way to get started is to check with your county Cooperative Extension Service about programs and classes or just talk with an agent. They offer intensive Master Gardener classes, and the Master Gardeners are happy to work with interested gardeners. Many extension services and/or Master Gardeners have newsletters and publications teaching others about gardening in their areas. They can also tell you about houseplants and caring for them.

Before you jump into gardening, you do need to ask yourself several questions:

1. Why do I want to do this? If you have the thought that you can grow flowers or vegetables cheaper than you can buy them, perish the thought. If gardening is to

be part of your meditative or spiritual life, that should be the primary motivation.

2. If I am to use this as a meditative and reflective practice, am I going to be able to focus on the doing of it and not on having some kind of showcase garden or plant or terrarium? The risk with gardening is that, like so many leisure projects, it takes on some aspects of a job, and the results can become too much an expression of ego and, often, an old competitive instinct ("Can you believe the size of my tomatoes?").

3. How much time do I want to spend at it? This will determine how large a garden or how many house-plants.

4. Do I want to grow vegetables? If so, which ones? If you have any spot of ground that receives at least six hours of sun a day, you can grow a tomato plant. And if you've never done it, you'll be amazed at how many tomatoes one plant can produce. Vegetables do require sun and space.

5. Is this something I can share with my spouse or life partner? Would I want to, or would I prefer this to be a solitary activity for me?

If you answer these questions satisfactorily and decide to take the next steps, you are in for a wonderful adventure. Believe me, the rewards are great indeed. In fact, I can't think of a pastime that offers as much return on so little investment of money and time.

And I've never met a gardener who was like those stereotypical sitcom characters. They're not inclined to be grouchy and irascible; more likely they are almost joyful in their relationship with the primal elements of soil and seeds and plants.

JOHN AND HOLLY'S STORY

Finding Spirit Whatever You Do, Wherever You Go

John and Holly Clark say they don't work at infusing their lives with spirituality. Rather, they play at it.

"It may sound weird when I say it," says Holly, "but when I see a squirrel running across the street, it makes me laugh, and I say, 'Thank God for squirrels.' I'm intensely aware of my spirituality when I'm happy. You've heard of getting a rush? That's how spiritual makes me feel."

John and Holly are baby boomers. He is vice president of finance and oversees human resources for a medical foundation; she is an adjunct instructor at a local college. They have a son graduating from college soon.

John does not plan to work until the standard retirement age, and Holly will be ready to retire when John is. They don't think about retirement a lot, but their general goals are to accumulate enough dollars that "making a living is less important than making a life."

Unlike many professional people of his age, John believes he does not identify himself by his job title or his job description. "I understand that for each of us, a portion of who we are is shaped by our work experiences, but only a portion. Sometimes we can spend so much energy at developing our careers early in life that we forget what we wanted to do with the career once we achieved success, . . . and sometimes we forget about the other aspects of our lives that are equally important to our personal development. . . . Aging and retirement have a way of reminding us that successes are stops on the journey and not destinations, and aging encourages us to change and continue to progress. . . . When you identify too much with the job title, you sometimes lose sight of other opportunities for contribution and growth. Retirement can offer that opportunity if we are not too attached to past successes.

"I don't find as much meaning in my work as I used to," he continues, "yet I really try to help the staff of thirty-five-plus that I work with understand that they're making an important contribution, in our case, to health care. But I don't want to be known as a vice president of finance. Even when I travel, I never talk about my job specifically. People on airliners always ask one another, 'What do you do?' I never say my title. If I were to say vice president, that builds a barrier with some people. If I say accountant, that sends an image of a left-brain nerd. So I say where I live, that I'm happily married and have a twenty-two-year-old son. Unfortunately, people have trouble with that because they can't categorize me.

"So I don't think I'll have a loss of identity at retirement because I haven't answered that what-do-you-do question for twenty years by giving my job title, the company I work for, and so on."

John compares himself to his son Ryan. "He's worried about what he's going to do after he graduates from college, whether he'll be successful, how he'll establish himself. I'm somewhat in the same position. I've done all kinds of things in my life—driven taxis, kept books for a trucking company, taken wedding photographs for a studio, sold advertising, prepared tax returns, been an auditor, headed a personnel department, been a waiter. So I don't know what I'll do when I retire. I may have some kind of job, but it will not be about money; it will be about doing something that has meaning for me and for other people, will provide spiritual growth, and, most important, keep Holly and me growing as a couple."

John and Holly are passionate about their deep connection, and they imbue it with a great deal of meaning. For instance, John emphasizes "energy" as part of his feelings of spirituality, and Holly asserts that they feel their energies are connected. "Sometimes when I'm feeling down," she says, "just his presence gives me energy. I feel energized. I truly feel that we enhance one another's spirituality."

"We don't start out to do it," John says. "It's not intentional but it comes out that way. Our intent is to work on our own, but the outcome is that the other person helps. This is probably due to the fact that we enjoy being together so much. We even run errands together. As for enhancing one another's spirituality, we don't work at it; we just play at it, and it happens."

They have had an on-again, off-again relationship with the church. They come from families closely connected with church; in fact, they met at church. "But we're sort of on a sabbatical from church," John says.

"Every once in a while, we think we ought to go back, but we are getting our spiritual needs met outside the church," John says. Holly responds, "I'm on a slightly different page on this subject. I don't feel the need to go back to church. In fact, I'm feeling rebellious about the church. It's a personal thing and I'm not trying to influence anyone else's thinking about that, but sometimes I think there's not really a church that worships my God."

So how does she define her God? "I'm working on that. I definitely believe in God, but I guess I'm a work in progress on that subject."

John adds, "I think you can be spiritual and not religious, and you can be religious and not spiritual. I feel Holly and I are just as involved in congregational worship as if we were going to church. We don't have to be in a church in a pew. In fact, recently the number of people who want to discuss and explore spirituality with us has surprised us, . . . or maybe we are more open to listening."

They insist that spirituality and their spiritual journeys are focal points of their retirement planning just as spiritual considerations are a focal point of their present lives, including daily meditation, reading, and even their travel.

One of the ways they get their spiritual needs met is by reading. John, who, Holly says, is a frustrated thespian, reads to her regularly. "He's a good reader, too," she says. After every reading, they discuss the material, which ranges from books by Deepak Chopra to Joseph Campbell to Bryan Greene, Scott Peck, Marcus Borg, Gary Zukav, and Marilyn Ferguson. "Most of our reading has a spiritual theme of one sort or another."

Their travel planning and traveling itself focus on the attitude and intention they bring to the trip and not on the trip alone. They begin by reading everything they can find about the places they want to visit. Not just tour guides, but some history and commentary. "We do a lot of preparation," John says, "which is part of it. We try to put more meaning into travel than just seeing sights."

"And while we bring back one memorable souvenir from every trip, usually a Christmas tree ornament," adds Holly, "they are not shopping trips; they're experience trips. And we never took a trip that was not just wonderful, even a simple drive along the Mississippi River to St. Louis."

John points out that they both come from humble backgrounds. "So we

"We want to travel with fresh eyes, we want to experience a place and its people and not just observe them."

never in our lives anticipated having the chance to go to Europe. Traveling to and in Europe is—to us, anyway—a major deal. We love the whole process, reading about places, about people, about history. We particularly like

229

to get out of the big cities and into the countryside, to places where there are fewer tourists. We know we can't really connect at a deep level with people in that context, but we like to make opportunities to be with local people, to try to experience them in some small way."

What are they trying to learn, if anything?

"We find that travel broadens our way of thinking and how we approach the world. We want to travel with fresh eyes, we want to experience a place and its people and not just observe them. We realize there are many different cultural approaches to life and that ours is not necessarily right or wrong. We're interested in how we approach our lives versus what it would be like if we'd been born in the place we're visiting. We look for the chance to try on different backgrounds for a while. It's difficult. We don't really feel connected; on the other hand, we also don't exactly feel like outsiders looking in."

There's another factor that always goes into making a trip wonderful: "Just being together, having the opportunity to talk about our everyday lives, long periods of silence. Times like that."

PART FIVE

Time for Your Inner Self

JUST AS THE demands of our work lives can make us lose touch with family and friends, so can we lose touch with our own inner lives. Even if we have regularly attended a place of worship, we often have put that experience into the category of something else on the calendar to get done this week. True, some of us may be among those admirably disciplined people who have, with deliberation and intention, maintained a strongly focused and centered spiritual practice. But alas, most of us have let those intentions atrophy under the pressure of the work life.

When in my lectures and workshops in organizations all over the country I stress the importance of "nurturing the inner life," I hasten to explain that the inner life is nurtured in many ways, from quiet times with family and friends to participation in the arts, either doing them or appreciating them, to leisure activities done in a meditative or reflective way. This more conscious way of being in life should be a fundamental goal of a retirement of personal growth and meaning, and indeed much of this book has already addressed this subject as a part of other subjects.

> *The inner life is nurtured in many ways, from quiet times with family and friends to participation in the arts.*

In this section, however, are two chapters of specific ways to enrich the inner life. The first suggests that you look inside yourself to find or rekindle areas of creativity you may have abandoned or postponed during the working years. The second offers possibilities for intensely spiritual practices, activities, and retreats.

Interspersed, of course, are stories of people who are in one way or another focusing energy and attention on nurturing the inner life.

JEANNA'S STORY
You Can Plan for the Spiritual

Jeanna Collins grew up in the small town of Baxley, Georgia, became a public school teacher who studied and taught abroad, and was honored with numerous awards. Yet she says that in the past twenty years her professional achievements, career, and money making have always been secondary to her search for spiritual and personal growth.

For those who think the words *spiritual* and *planning* don't go together, Jeanna has a viewpoint you should hear. "I would advise people definitely to make plans," she says, "because the process of planning forces you to define what is spiritual to you, what is important to do with the rest of your life, and helps establish priorities." Plan, define, establish priorities. Not words we usually associate with a spiritual journey, but Jeanna is able to bring these together because her own paths to spirituality have been so many and diverse.

"The keyword for me is *journey*," she says. "Regardless of the path I'm currently on, I always think of it as a pilgrimage to a place, moment, reflection, insight that enlivens me in some way and draws me to the Divine, however I have understood the Divine at that time. Some of the paths I've taken through the years that have given me those epiphany moments have included an intense study of Hildegard of Bingen, the twelfth-century

233

Rhineland mystic; an involvement with Holocaust education with eighth graders, which resulted in beautiful poetry by students as well as the creation of a permanent memorial for the children of the Holocaust; and painful trips to the camps in Poland.

"My conversion to Catholicism, particularly with the Communion of Saints, which is so meaningful to me, is another path, frustrating at times with its misogyny and right-wing politics but continuing to heal through the beauty and depth of the ritual.

"The works of Joseph Campbell, with their emphasis on comparative mythology, have led me down another path, which resulted in the establishment of a mythological roundtable with a wonderful group of people. That group still meets. Campbell's ideas about the 'oneness' of all things and his insistence that 'it is here' that we find the Divine in ourselves, in others, and in the world are definitely a part of my idea of spirituality."

Some of the paths and influences continue to influence Jeanna and were part of her consciousness as she began to make her plans for retirement.

She made three big plans. The first was a walking tour to Santiago, Spain, on the old medieval pilgrimage route. She read several books by seekers of spirituality, not necessarily Christian, who walked The Way, as it is called. She also read "a wonderful book about seeing all trips as a pilgrimage. I knew each landmark to look for and had special prayers requested by friends to offer along the way."

Her second plan was to become more involved in a woman's circle group in which she had participated for several months while studying the book *The Alphabet vs. the Goddess*. "I found that the incredible energy as well as a deep sense of peace studying with women was very stimulating and put me in touch with the feminine aspects of the Divine that I have been seeking. I'm rather a latecomer to my femininity since I grew up with no father and very strong women. I plunged headfirst into a man's world determined to conquer. I've since discovered the strength of the feminine and the dire need in our world for the balance of masculine and feminine."

Jeanna's third plan for retirement was to write. "I envisioned myself on the screened porch during the early mornings reflecting and writing. I bought a very nice journal that I saved for that first day when retirement officially began."

Jeanna felt her planning was "right on" concerning her deepest interests and needs. But things didn't go as planned. First there was September 11, 2001. In the aftermath of that event, most of the people scheduled to go on the walking trip in Spain backed out, the tour company filed bankruptcy, and Jeanna lost the $3,000 it had taken several years to save. This and the general despair of the nation at large after 9/11 threw her into a bit of a tailspin.

"I didn't really feel like writing, physical pilgrimage was out until I could save more money again, and I also found that not working was going to require a bit of adjusting that I really had not expected. I didn't miss work at all, but the change in the structure of the day caused me some problems with using my time efficiently.

> *"If you truly seek the spiritual, you may find it in a totally different place or in another way than the one you anticipated."*

"Obviously the problems with my plans had their impact, but I really think at this point I would have experienced some of the uncomfortable feelings under any circumstances. Regardless of your mind-set, you don't just walk away from thirty-four years of a certain way of life and not expect to go through some times of doubt, questioning, fear, lack of confidence, lack of feeling useful, realization of your life coming to an end, and so on."

Jeanna suspects a lot of newly retired people have these feelings and warns that they can lead to a point of doing less and less instead of more and more. It can put you in a funk.

Her response, once again, was to plan. She made herself plan for each day so that the time would not slip away. Her advice to others is to become aware that sometimes your plans just won't work exactly as you expect, and you have to "be flexible and flow with the stream. If you truly seek the spiritual, you may find it in a totally different place or in another way than the one you anticipated. That doesn't mean the plans were of no use. Planning, whether it works out or not, is a part of the process of change, and retirement is definitely a big change."

Jeanna has found a spiritual path within the wreckage of her unrealized plans. "The Spirit works best out of chaos," she says, "since your plans get in Her or His way. So I guess my upset plans are really going to serve me well in the long run. Although I'm still agonizing a bit over my disappointments, I am slowly beginning to realize that what will come out of these lost plans will be a better plan and that the Divine I seek is a part of all of this.

"I am finding a much greater realization of being a pilgrim in the everyday events as well as with the wonderful people in the study groups, women groups, and family groups that are here in my own backyard. Enter Dorothy and Toto! I've found myself reevaluating what it is that I really want to pursue spiritually and find that it's okay to allow some time without having to be 'on a schedule spiritually.' I find just focusing on what I have done and how I can bring many of the strands of my paths together into one many-layered strand is comforting and energizing."

Jeanna is starting to write in her journal. She plans to take a "Centering Prayer" workshop at a monastery and will sign up for Eucharistic Adoration once a week. In

September she plans to attend a Woman's Spirit Rising retreat at a monastery.

As an additional spiritual pursuit, she plays clarinet with a wind ensemble that performs three times a year and plans to attend more operas with her husband. She feels she is on track to complete some of the plans she made, though they have been adjusted somewhat.

The underlying focus of all this activity is her journey. "The only thing with real meaning for me is my search for the spiritual, so even if my path has a few bumps and curves, I know I'm still on a pilgrimage of spirituality, which to me means entering for a brief moment into 'eternity.' I believe that eternity is not 'to come' but is here and now, and our struggle as human beings is to catch a glimpse of that eternal moment, to see in that moment the interconnectedness of all things and to experience that oneness at the deepest level.

"Surely if more of us could do that, we would not be destroying other humans, the animals, the plant life, the Earth. . . . I am a practicing Catholic . . . and I find great riches in the church, but spirituality encompasses so much more than what we call religion."

CHAPTER ELEVEN

Expressing Your Creative Spirit

I BEGAN TO play the clarinet when I was in the seventh grade. Well, "play the clarinet" might be an overstatement. Actually, I was given a clarinet to carry but not actually play as I marched along in uniform. I was among those students whose job it was to look like a member of the band in order to make the spectators at the parade or football game think the band was actually bigger than it was. In other words, I was "padding."

I was embarrassed by that role, so I asked the band director whether I could actually learn to play. He gave me a book and a reed, and I taught myself. By the time I was in high school, I had my own dance band ("Jimmy Autry and the Tech High Swingsters"), auditioned for and was selected to play in the all-state concert band, and was talking to various colleges about music scholarships.

It was then that I, age seventeen and trying to sound adult, began to demonstrate my Depression and World War II influences by saying things like, "I love music, but I need to do something to put bread and butter on the table, so I'm going to major in journalism." So much for a music career.

> *Retirement provides us opportunities to do all those creative things we might have done earlier in life but abandoned or thought we'd never do again.*

But I'm back, playing clarinet again these days, and the reason is simple: I now have time to do it. Indeed, retirement provides us opportunities to do all those creative things we might have done earlier in life but abandoned or thought we'd never do again.

Several of the people I interviewed were embracing creative activities they'd long since left behind or ones they'd always wanted to try but never thought they had the time or talent. Some of them had lived most of their lives thinking, as one put it, "I don't have a creative bone in my body."

The good news is that the only person you have to satisfy creatively is yourself. There are no more bosses, no more deadlines, no more productivity standards to worry about. There is no one to judge the quality of your work except you yourself. Besides, the joy of personal growth is not so much in the finished work but in the doing of it, in the act of creation.

Resurrecting the Artist Within

Bert Hill is either a retired Air Force colonel who plays the trumpet and sings or a trumpet player and singer who retired from the Air Force. Either way, Bert has rediscovered not only his love of music but his love of singing and his talent for the trumpet, a talent nurtured first in public school.

After retiring several years ago, Bert began to play and sing again regularly, jamming with friends and honing his musical skills. And now he "gigs" with various jazz bands around his home and surrounding states, traveling miles for a one-night stand just as bands used to do back when he was in high school.

His explanation of how he was able to go from military officer to jazz musician is simple: "If retirement is about anything," he says, "it's about having more time. I am able to practice regularly. I had a great career, but they didn't give me a lot of time for the trumpet in Vietnam or at the Air War College."

JULIE GAMMACK, A former newspaper columnist and Internet entrepreneur now living on the East Coast, has after many years begun to paint again. She says, "In all those years, the artist within was hibernating. And now it is so liberating and freeing—and maybe this is part of the maturation process—to let go of the what-people-think syndrome . . . because you get to an age or a stage when you realize that none of that really matters in the end."

When Julie was in the fifth grade, her art teacher singled her out for a scholarship to take classes at the local art center. From that she went to private lessons with a teacher who inspired her enough that she considered attending the Kansas City Art Institute. She decided against it, explaining, "I'm not sure what it was, but I think the message was that art was something to do as a hobby, not a career." I could relate to that.

Julie even got to the point of feeling that "with all the poverty, racism, and war in the world, drawing and painting were frivolous wastes of time.

"So this painting thing remained dormant for most of twenty years. . . . The interest was always there, though, and periodically I'd pick up materials and try to go back to it, but it was frustrating more often than not because I'd forgotten so much or had never gotten the training for what I wanted to paint at the time."

In interview after interview, I found stories similar to Julie's, of people who had played an instrument in school or who had been a student artist or actor or sculptor, who had done crafts from cross-stitch to woodworking, but who had let that gift atrophy under the pressures of family and work life.

I asked Julie how she got started again. "I took a look at what was keeping me from art," she says, "and came to see that I needed to allow myself to be a 'beginner' again in order to learn what I needed to learn. Being willing to be a beginner was a big step."

Julie's reconnection with her art brought her to one of those synchronicities that seem always to happen when we're open to the possibilities. She and her mate, Richard, were shopping for some nautical art for the wall of their condo and found that the price tags for any original work were daunting, $6,000 to $10,000.

"Richard is a true Chesapeake sailor," she says, "and when I learned what kind of art he was drawn to, I decided to try it myself. The first risk was in buying a maritime chart for $18, which is a lot to pay for a 'canvas.' I bought a set of pastels and began to paint Richard's own boat superimposed on a Chesapeake chart.

"It was a huge risk. I expected it not to turn out and figured I'd be out the money for the chart and the pastels, which are not cheap, and the whole thing would go into a closet."

But it was a success. Then Julie was asked to paint a similar one for a friend of Richard. "Suddenly, the creator was set free."

She began to go to boat shows with samples of her work, and almost suddenly, it seems, she is in demand as an artist. "I still have a lot to learn," she says, "and there are times I clutch when I think of the orders I have to fill.

That's when I go for a walk in a lovely little park and have a conversation with God.

"What started happening to me at this stage of life," she concludes, "is that I find I'm far more open to taking risks and trusting the path of synchronicity. And there is a spiritual underpinning to those times when creation flows. Isn't it interesting to think about the connection between the words *creator* and *Creator?*"

EVEN THOUGH A creative outlet may turn into a money-making enterprise, it's not really about money. You can feel just as creative when you're expressing your spirit for no one but you. A forty-five-year-old single mom I know loved her jazz and ballet lessons and dance routines when she was younger. Now when her teenage sons are busy or asleep—in other words, when no one will see her—she puts on old albums of show tunes or just good music with a beat, and she does a simulation of her old routines or improvises however she feels. She claims that her dancing is a bit stiff and nowhere near as fluid as it once was, but her heart feels lighter, her mind clearer, and her spirit full of ideas and joy not only when she's dancing but for days afterward.

Finding a Talent You Didn't Know You Had

Ray Crawford was in the auto parts business most of his life, most recently as an owner of a salvage yard.

His wife, Martha Lynn Crawford, is a retired school-teacher.

About two years ago, Martha, who had always been drawn to writing and painting, decided to try pottery as a hobby, something she had never done or even considered doing. She started small, as most people do, then expanded to various pieces. She worked for herself, family, and friends, with no intention of selling her work. It was strictly a labor of love and a powerful creative outlet.

You can probably figure out what happened next. People who'd heard of her work began to show up at her door and offer to buy the pottery. Encouraged, she began to place a few pieces in a local gift shop. One led to another and then another until finally Martha bought not only a professional potter's wheel but also a larger kiln.

Ray, who had already begun to help with the firing of the pots, became interested in creating a few pieces himself. "I don't know, I just seemed to have a knack for doing some of it," he says. "Of course, Martha does the really creative things."

The demand became so great that Ray and Martha made a major life decision. Ray would pull slowly away from the salvage business—"Business was slowing down anyway," he points out—and they would try to turn the pottery into a full-time business.

"We don't intend to become big with a bunch of employees or anything like that," Martha says. "We want to keep it to a size that we can continue to enjoy the creative work without feeling that we're under pressure to produce more and more and more all the time. The main thing for us is that we do good work and enjoy it at the same time."

Ray and Martha are devout Christians who determined that their new success was a blessing from God and that their pottery creations also offered them an opportunity for ministry. So they named their products "Vessels of Honour," and they sign and date each piece along with a reassuring comment and a reference for a Bible verse. A favorite is "Don't give up. Keep going! Isaiah 40:31."

Martha explains that "it just seemed like something we should do. We've had our share of difficulties in life, and we just want to encourage other people."

Will they ever finally retire for sure? "This *is* retirement," Ray says.

Think Creatively

Probably nothing in retirement offers such endless opportunities for personal and spiritual growth as looking inside yourself and discovering, or rediscovering, the creator within. We all have something within us worth bringing to creative fruition and sharing with others.

Your place of worship is a good resource. There are choirs; if you're not a singer, there are bell choirs, and you don't even have to read music to play the bells. There are crafts groups that create wall hangings and decorations for various seasons of the worship calendar.

246

Almost every city or medium-size town has a writer's or poet's group. There are storytelling groups for those with active imaginations or entertaining recollections. Journaling, an often-used therapeutic tool, can also be a source of creativity. The writing may never get turned into a book or be seen by anyone but yourself, but it will unlock your creative spirit and be an outlet of sheer expression.

There are community theater groups for aspiring actors or costume designers or set workers. There are art centers with classes for people at every level, from beginner to accomplished artist.

We all have something within us worth bringing to creative fruition and sharing with others.

Adult education programs in most communities also offer a slew of artistic endeavors: photography, flower arranging, origami, basket weaving, papermaking, scrapbooking, woodworking, carving, stained glass, and other crafts.

CREATIVITY HAS ALMOST become an overused word in our society, to the point that it begins to lose its meaning. The important thing to know is that your creativity can be expressed in anything from dressing up in colors or outfits that are different from your regular attire, to putting together and cooking a great menu or throwing a party. Actually, anything you do that's out of your ordinary pattern and that releases that feeling of pure joy at being alive is creative.

Whatever you choose to do, you should not worry about how well you do it, only that you enjoy it. In interviews with people who had once been involved as an artist, writer, craftsperson, or musician, I found again and again a reluctance to give it another try. The most common responses were "I've forgotten everything I ever knew about it," or "I couldn't even make a sound on that horn now," or something similar. In other interviews, people who'd never been involved in a creative endeavor often confessed that they'd had a lifelong desire to do something "artistic" but thought it was now too late.

The reasons for not doing it, now that they have the time, were often about age-related physical conditions: stiff fingers or problems with eyesight or hearing or mobility. These are real concerns, to be sure, but I also found people with similar problems who clearly felt that their enjoyment of a creative activity was not diminished simply because they could no longer perform to the standard they once achieved or couldn't attain the proficiency of a younger person. Although there clearly are physical deterrents to all kinds of arts endeavors, from playing an instrument to painting to dancing, it often seemed to me that, in some of these interviews, the difference was more one of attitude than infirmity.

An alternative to doing the art yourself, of course, is simply appreciating the arts: attending concerts and theatrical performances, going to galleries, tuning into the arts channels on television, listening to CDs. Remember that the appreciator is also a creative participant in the arts. The artist's work is only half the equation; without someone to receive and appreciate the finished creation, the artist works in something of a vacuum. There are those rare artists who wish to keep their work to themselves or a small circle of admirers, but most artists not only are generous in wanting to share what they do but also are fed creatively by the appreciation and response.

So creativity is a two-way street, and in one form or another, it is somewhere within each of us. In simply searching for it, we open ourselves to one of the most rewarding paths of spiritual growth. As Julie Gammack said, there's an interesting parallel in the words *creator* and *Creator*. Indeed, our instinct toward creativity in all its forms may well be the most widespread evidence of what writers and poets, philosophers and theologians have referred to as the "Divine spark."

DRAKE'S STORY
Cultivate the Relationship with Spirit and Soul

Drake Sadler, the CEO of Traditional Medicinals, a tea company that he cofounded twenty-eight years ago, once had a conversation about spiritual practice with one of his employees.

"I don't have a spiritual practice," said the man.

Then Drake asked, "Don't you coach Little League?"

"Yes," the employee replied. "I do that several times a week. I love those kids."

"How many hours a week does that amount to?" Drake asked.

"Oh, probably ten or sometimes twelve hours a week."

"In that case," Drake said, "you have more spiritual practice than 90 percent of the people in the world."

After telling me this story, Drake said, "I just don't know how people operate in this world without a strong spiritual foundation. I can only guess they make their way unconsciously through the pain and suffering of life."

Drake's own spiritual practice began with a dream in the early seventies. "In all my dreams there appeared a spiritual figure standing over me, with sort of an ethereal look."

He did not know what the dream meant or what the figure represented. Then a woman Drake was dating at the time gave him a book, *The Autobiography of a Yogi* by Yogananda. On the cover was a figure whom Drake recognized as the figure in his dreams. He opened the book and began to read. It changed his life forever.

"As soon as I read the first paragraph, I had this overwhelming feeling of being at home, a feeling I'd never had before, like a deep stirring and a sense of security."

Drake had been raised as a "progressive Christian." The people around him, including his parents, were "good people, honest people with good values," but they went to church irregularly.

Before the dream and the experience of reading Yogananda's book, Drake had practiced meditation and explored his consciousness in many different ways, including visiting retreats and experimenting with "a lot of stuff of the day, like est and Mind Dynamics and others." But none of it satisfied him like Yogananda.

"From the very beginning I was struck with the feeling that this was to be my spiritual teacher. There was never a question in my mind about following his path and his teachings. I decided that even in my limited capacity I was going to try to live the life of a yogi.

"Yogananda gave me what I needed. He was a very practical, follow-these-steps kind of teacher. That appealed to me because I am a process person. I want to go from A to Z."

In the back of Yogananda's autobiography was a section on contacting his organization, how to get more information, and other books to read. Drake began to absorb everything Yogananda had written.

"I got to the point that I just knew in the core of my being that this was a man who knew God. I trusted what he said, and I trusted that I could have that same experience of God. I've been a devout follower ever since. And you have to realize that for me, a guy who's independent and strong-willed and doesn't always listen very well, this was a big leap for me. But it was the best leap I ever made."

Though devoted to Yogananda's spiritual practice, Drake has continued to explore various philosophies and religions. He has studied the books of spiritual writers, practiced Buddhist meditations, and gone on meditation retreats, but the primary focus of his spiritual practice remains around Yogananda's teachings.

"Yogananda basically provided me with an operating system, involving right attitude, the way I approach my life, right livelihood, right diet, as well as meditation, values, ethics, and principles."

Drake explains that there are eight different types of yogas. "The one most people talk about is the 'hatha yoga,' the one involving physical exercise. But understand that *yoga* means 'union,' so the yogic path is the path of union with God. And there are different ways to experience that union. Another one people talk about is 'karma yoga,' the path wherein you create only good karma by doing goodwill. This means that all of your thinking, your actions, must be done without harm and only to create positive results in the world. A good example of karmic yoga would be Habitat for Humanity or the work of Mother Teresa. She was creating good in the world by service in every thought and action and deed. She was a Catholic, of course, but in the yogic sense she was a karma yogi."

I asked Drake to explain how this works in the "real world" of business and work. "You're a CEO," I said. "You have employees and customers and vendors and competitors. How does a yogi run a business?"

"It doesn't matter if you're talking about work and business or home and family," he responded, "whether you're retired or still working. It's the same. The old belief was that, in order to know God, you had to be a celibate monk, walk around with a loincloth and a begging bowl, or something like that. But in the last century, spiritual leaders began to promote the idea that everyone could become God-conscious or self-realized through discipline and devotion.

"If we are going to change the world for the better, we must have modern-day yogis who operate in the world, who bring spiritual practice into the world, and not retreat from the world. The practice is as simple as being honest and forthright, caring for people, living modestly, and not becoming attached to the window dressings of life or the outcomes of our actions."

Drake has been attending the same week-long meditation retreat for twenty-five years. It offers classes, lectures, long periods of meditation, singing, chanting, and fellowship. "The interesting thing about this annual retreat," he says, "is that when I'm there I reach a point during the week that I feel it's as if the whole rest of the year revolves around that week, as if the rest of the fifty-one weeks is a dream. And for one week I'm awake again and completely present. That's how profound a week of focused introspection can be."

While he believes that spiritual retreats can be beneficial for anyone, he also insists that "it's important to set time aside every day for God, to develop a personal relationship with God. And it's important to set aside time to cultivate this relationship with spirit and soul, with the inner life. You don't have to go on a retreat to do that."

What About Retirement?

Drake sees the second half of his life becoming more interiorized. "As I move more toward an inner life, my spiritual practice will deepen, with fewer worldly duties and responsibilities."

He has no regrets about having devoted so much of his life to the tea company, but in retrospect is able to see how much he has sacrificed on a personal level to participate in business. "I'd never do it differently," he says. "It's been great, but I do realize the sacrifice. Retirement for me does not necessarily mean leaving business all together, because there are aspects I absolutely love and are vehicles for experiencing God in my life."

But he will increase the time given to community and personal service. He sits on the board of the local Community Action Program, which manages Head Start schools, homeless and battered women shelters, drug programs, youth programs, and other issues facing low-income families and people at risk. "All that is part of the path of selfless service."

Drake ended our interview by talking about the philosophy of his life and work: "If my work in the world doesn't serve my community and the people who work at our company and their families . . . if it doesn't reach all of those people, then I'm not fulfilling my commitment to a spiritual life and to God."

LEX'S STORY
Golf as a Spiritual Discipline

Lex Alexander, who retired early from a large natural products supermarket chain, has calling cards that read, "The Food Guy," but this is only how he still wants to be known to the outside world. On the inside, he thinks of himself as "the golf guy."

"I admit it," he says. "I see myself more than anything else as a golfer, but, unfortunately, I find that the venue in which golf is so often played, the country club, is an environment whose values I don't want to be surrounded with. In fact, if you mention golf to most people, even those who play the game, they get this image of plaid pants, golf carts, and perhaps beer.

"I am pursuing golf as a spiritual practice. People have a yoga practice or tai chi practice or a Zen practice, but no one usually speaks of golf as a spiritual practice. Most people would probably think that the game is the farthest thing possible from a spiritual practice, yet that's exactly what it is to me."

Lex insists that, in the spiritual sense, golf is like a minilife. "In our fast-paced culture, one of the complaints about golf is that it takes too long, but to me one of the intriguing parts is that it takes a long time. I walk. I feel that connection with the earth for over five miles. The golfer is essentially alone. If you play by the rules, if you walk instead of ride a cart, you can feel the complete experience, and just as in life, you'll have good breaks and bad breaks, disappointment and exhilarating joy.

"There's a quote from *Golf in the Kingdom* by Michael Murphy that goes, 'Ye'll come away from the links with a new hold on life, that is certain if ye play the game with all your heart.'

"The game is so metaphysical to me because it requires all of me. When it goes well, the voice I hear and the person I perceive myself to be come together in me. When it's not going well, they still seem to come together but in a different way."

Lex points out that the nature of the game itself is what provides the potential for spiritual experience. "Think about the ball itself," he says. "In most sports

If you play by the rules, if you walk instead of ride a cart, you can feel the complete experience, and just as in life, you'll have good breaks and bad breaks, disappointment and exhilarating joy.

you're reacting to the ball. You can even blame the other side or the other person for what they did to the ball before you got it. But in golf, the ball is still until you hit it. You project that ball away from yourself, and wherever it goes is where you have sent it. No one will send it back, as in tennis. What makes all this so metaphysical is that you have to blend the mind and body together at this particular instant in time in order to project this object away from yourself.

"I hit a shot six months ago that, because of the light and the landscape, I could see for 255 yards against the sky. Very few things in my life are that exhilarating or fulfilling or make me feel so at one with myself and with the environment.

"And then add this factor: In some sports, the harder you try, the harder you train, the better shape you're in physically, the better performance you get. But in golf you have to hit that fine balance between trying too hard and not trying at all. Fulfillment comes from not getting in your own way."

Lex does not suggest that he's always at peace and always in the right spiritual place when he's on a golf course. To the contrary, he points out that the game can be emotionally brutal. "One of the things that makes golf a reflective practice is the scoring system. It's so finite and everyone understands it, but people are always looking for comfort from one another: 'That's okay—your putt is good.' There's no referee to call a foul or penalty; you're on your honor to know the rules and play by them and record your score. In some ways, that finite aspect is part of the spiritual practice I'm seeking."

Regardless of his insistence on honorable scorekeeping, winning is not what drives Lex. "I have to work at that, but I struggle not to focus on the end result but to focus on the process of the journey, being conscious of who I am out there. This is another way that golf can be a metaphor for life."

In his younger years, Lex was a golf pro. He says he was a better teacher than golfer, but he realized that he'd prefer to play rather than teach. And though he has retired at a relatively young age, he doesn't plan to go back to work. "I get tempted to go back to work because I'm good at it, but I really want to accept this retirement and build this relationship with golf."

I asked Lex whether, since golf is like life, he ever gets angry or frustrated while playing. "I do, and I think that's also part of the journey, part of what I have to learn to deal with. I have this image of myself as a southern gentleman who has good manners and does the right thing, but my shadow self is most accessible to me in this game of golf because I find a rage that is sometimes expressed, and I can't ignore it. It expresses itself in my disappointment or sometimes in tantrums."

Lex tells about a day in which he hit a bad shot and became so angry he destroyed an umbrella that was attached to his golf bag.

"I would like it if that part of me didn't exist, but it's fascinating to realize that it's in there and I have to recognize it. Trying to deal with it has a lot to do with managing expectations, honoring the process, and not being so tied into the results.

"On my good days, I can connect with the trees and the sunshine and can let go of that need to control. In those times the voice that says to me, 'This is an important shot; don't screw it up,' tends to fall away. Recognizing this shadow side leads me to strive to hit that peak experience."

And what form does that striving take?

"I try to play without fear of failure. I tell myself that my family's not in peril; no one's going to take my money away; no one's going to reassign me to live in a trailer park. It's just a game. But I still have trouble sometimes, because somehow the chance of embarrassment at missing the short putt or not making it over the water with the six iron produces fear. I have to confront that fear. In other sports, you can always rationalize that the other team played well, but the game of golf is unforgivable in that way.

"My goal, which I am able to achieve some of the time, is to be able to screw up and still feel that connection with the sun and the Earth, and still be able to honor the process itself."

Lex does not claim that he will achieve this goal completely but only that working at it, being conscious of the goal and of who he is at all times, is part of what makes the game a spiritual discipline for him.

"What I'm attempting to do now in the next few years is to make sense of the game in the context of a spiritual practice. I've been tempted to go back into teaching in order to articulate this expression of the game.

"But I ask myself, 'What if someone told me I have eighteen months to live?' There's no question what I'd do with that time. Play golf. So that's the answer of what to do right now."

.

CHAPTER TWELVE

Connecting with Soul and Spirit

IF ONE THING is certain, it is that in order to enjoy the freedoms and opportunities that retirement life can offer, those very benefits you've worked so hard for all these years, you have to take care of yourself. You have to see to your own health and well-being physically, psychologically, emotionally, and spiritually.

We have ubiquitous reminders everywhere in our society about the importance of nutrition and exercise in helping you maintain some of the energy and vigor you need to participate in an active life, so there's no need for this book to add to that vast amount of information.

But it needs to be said also that, while a healthy body can be an important contributor to psychological, emotional, and spiritual health, many people who are ill,

263

disabled, or restricted physically still enjoy abundantly rich inner lives. And that is the beauty of a life of spiritual growth: It is available to everyone in every economic circumstance and of every physical ability.

In my fervor and enthusiasm for the spiritual life, however, I don't kid myself. I know that some people live with such challenging conditions or in such repressive circumstances that they would consider "a life of spiritual growth" or "the spiritual path" or the "journey of the spirit"—phrases that have been used at one place or another in this book—to be the pretentious indulgences of people who don't have to worry about just staying alive or about where their next meal is coming from.

Just as maintaining a healthy body requires discipline and commitment, so does nurturing the inner life require discipline and commitment as well as self-awareness.

I believe that people of spirit must acknowledge this reality in order to keep their spiritual compasses aligned with the world. Thus, the stories in this book have focused on people who don't retreat from the world into a monastic existence (though there's nothing wrong with that, of course) but who involve themselves in spiritual disciplines and practices that they can then bring into the world for the benefit of the world.

For you to do this, you must be spiritually strong, and just as you take care of your physical body, so you must take care of, nurture, and strengthen your inner self. And just as maintaining a healthy body requires discipline and commitment, so does nurturing the inner life require discipline and commitment as well as self-awareness.

As you've read in the stories throughout this book, there are no predetermined techniques that, if practiced regularly, will guarantee a state of spiritual nirvana. To the contrary, spiritual growth is not an event, episode, or destination; it is a journey, and the growth takes place within the journey itself. Not only are there many paths, but you can even take several paths at the same time. Again, this has parallels with physical well-being. You may pump iron, jog, walk, swim, do aerobics, and so on, or you can combine those activities. No one of them is the single best way to condition your body. The same is true for spiritual conditioning. In fact, you can even combine your physical and spiritual practices. For example, most of the martial arts emphasize their ritual, spiritual, and physical aspects equally.

Many people are resistant to spiritual practices because of an assumed association in some areas of society with cults or esoteric sects. Other people may fear they'll be embarrassed or uncomfortable because the practices themselves require knowledge, physical agility, a certain body image, specific garments, or even a large commitment of time.

I don't believe in a hierarchy of spiritual experiences, and I don't believe they are limited by religious belief, creed, doctrine, or dogma. It is important to understand that, while the spiritual journey may lead you to a greater attitude of humility and gratitude, it requires neither your embarrassment nor your discomfort. Your inner life doesn't have to be nurtured by bending your body into certain postures or chanting or beating on drums, or eating only fruits and nuts, or drinking only goat's milk and honey. Yet, all of that could be part of a spiritual practice if you choose. If what you focus on is prayer, you can pray silently, or you can shout, pray alone, or pray in groups.

Your activities in the service of others can most assuredly be spiritual practices. Consider David Jordan's visits to the hospital to hold the premature babies. Perhaps he might not call that a spiritual practice, but if I were doing it, I would. A gathering of loving friends sharing their deepest selves is for me a spiritual practice, as is Jeanna Collins's mythological roundtable group. I consider Ken and Peg McDougall's service to the families of critically ill children to be a spiritual practice, as well as Marti Sivi's theatrical work in prison, and Virginia Traxler's work as a doula. Drake Sadler considers that his employee who coaches Little League twelve hours a week to be involved in a significant spiritual practice.

Whatever connects you with what so many spiritual leaders refer to as the "oneness" can be a path to spiritual growth. Just remember that the important thing is not the activity itself but the presence you bring to it. I exclude virtually nothing as long as it is done reflectively and meditatively: jogging, reading, participating in the arts, even golf, as you just read in Lex Alexander's story.

Carol Burns tries to make everything she does a spiritual practice. "Spirituality is part of my daily life. It's part of my whole person." Her journey has included traditional Christianity as well as investigations and studies of other world religions and philosophy. 'What am I seeking?" she asks, then answers, "Truth, a way to be thankful, meaning, understanding about the adventure we're all on. . . . I sometimes can't believe life itself because I find it so phenomenal."

In short, there are all kinds of religious and meditative practices, spiritual paths that have worked for many people. But there are no rules about how to achieve that connection, that transcendent feeling of being in the presence of the Divine. It depends entirely on you. The good news is that you're not on your own; not only are there many options, but many resources, teachers, and support organizations and groups are available as well.

You may even want to consider working with a spiritual director. Don't confuse this practice with therapy, although there are therapeutic aspects to it; and don't confuse this with ministry, either, though there are pastoral and ministerial aspects to it. You may work with a spiritual director individually, in a group, or both.

Cheryl Sypal tells of her great desire for a connection with others who were also on a spiritual path. "I one day said to God that I would provide the place if you would provide the people. Seven years later, these people are still meeting in my home. We met every other week for a while, but now meet once a month. We study books; we meditate and pray; we look at other traditions; we drum and chant, do rituals, and share our lives, fears, and failures. What a journey it has been for all of us.

"Along the way I met a spiritual director who counsels me on a regular basis and guides my spiritual direction. She also guides me in my understanding of dreams. I am in a spiritual direction group that meets about once a month for a similar practice."

Spiritual Practices: Prayer

In the more than twenty years that I have known him, my father-in-law, Gerald Pederson, has said a prayer before every meal. And he never fails to close the prayer with a request that epitomizes to me what so much of this book is about: "Bless this food," he says, "that it may strengthen us so we can serve you by serving others."

Probably the most widespread and accessible spiritual practice is prayer. There's nothing to it, yet there's everything to it. A minister friend once told me that if I just consciously think that I'd like to pray or that I should pray, then I've already prayed as far as God is concerned. A word prayer is only a way of putting into words for ourselves those things that God doesn't need words for.

So I asked the minister, "If that's true, if God already knows what's inside me and what I'm going to pray about, then why pray at all?"

"You don't say prayers for God to hear," he answered. "You say them for you to hear."

Then there are other kinds of prayer that not only don't use words but that don't even use imagery. Some call this "centering prayer" or "contemplative prayer." It reminds me of what I've heard of transcendental meditation, in that it is done by sitting in silence and trying to clear your mind completely of any thought.

Kay Riley, a spiritual director, says, "What means the most to me in centering prayer is the concept of resting in God, resting in the spirit. That means I don't have to do anything other than be aware of a spaciousness in me where God is present, and be open to it."

The concept of centering prayer is credited to Father Thomas Keating, a Cistercian priest, monk, and abbot at St. Benedictine Monastery in Snowmass, Colorado. Father Keating founded Contemplative Outreach, a center whose mission is "committed to living the contemplative dimension of the Gospel in everyday life through the practice of Centering Prayer." There are Contemplative Outreach chapters in nearly twenty states and in Canada and Guam. For a listing of chapters, instruction, and articles on centering prayer, plus information on retreats and support, see **www.contemplativeoutreach.org** or **www.centeringprayer.com.**

Father Keating has written many books on the subject of spirituality and prayer. *Open Mind, Open Heart: The Contemplative Dimension of the Gospel,* written in 1986, details the history of contemplative prayer and gives step-by-step guidance for centering prayer.

> *The more you engage in prayer of any type, the more you will want to explore ways to enrich the experience.*

There are many kinds of prayer—intercessionary, devotional, confessional, and so on—and some of the world's most renowned thinkers, philosophers, and theologians have written on the subject. Most of their work has to do with exploring the many intricate dimensions of this approach to the Divine, and the more you engage in prayer of any type, the more you will want to explore ways to enrich the experience.

Meditation

My friend Tom Gould tells me he prays twenty minutes every morning then follows that with twenty minutes of meditation.

"What's the difference?" I asked him.

"In the first, I go rather ritualistically through a list of beloved people in my life, and I ask that they be blessed in whatever they're doing. In meditation, I put everything out of my mind and just try to achieve a state of no thought, no images. Prayer is active participation in a conversation with God. Meditation is a journey into a place in which my mind is not involved."

Like so many spiritual experiences for which we struggle to find words, meditation is difficult to define. Plus, there are as many kinds of meditation as there are kinds of prayer. I know a man who practices "active meditation" in that, rather than sitting quietly with his eyes closed and mind empty, he tries to bring a meditative state to every activity.

"It requires that you be intentional about everything you do and experience it fully," he says. "That means that every meeting, every physical exercise, every conversation becomes the center of your focus and that you clear your mind in that moment of everything except that. You're not trying to shut down your thoughts; you're trying to bring more meaning into the moment regardless of what you're doing at that moment."

Even sitting meditation does not have to be a singular activity. Many Buddhists regularly "sit" together in what might be described as spiritual communion. Despite the silence, it is a very bonding experience. I have a Zen Buddhist friend who likes to recall with affection people he "used to sit with" years ago.

INTERNET RESOURCES: MEDITATION WEB SITES

The sources of information on meditation are almost too numerous to mention, but here are some to get you started. If you know what kind you're looking for, you can find information on that specific practice by searching www.google.com or searching for books and magazines with the key words.

www.meditationcenter.com is a worldwide online compendium of resources, guidance, techniques, and readings. The site is divided into rooms based on your purpose for meditating (laying a foundation, relieving stress, healing, and enlightenment). You can also write in questions that will be answered by Jim Malloy, the host and instructor who has more than twenty-five years of instruction all over the world. The site also offers meditation tapes for purchase.

www.meditationsociety.com, the site of the Meditation Society of America, posts information for beginners to experts and everyone in between, including techniques, concepts, and readings.

Meditation is, more than anything, being in the moment, each moment one at a time. Jon Kabat-Zinn, author of *Wherever You Go, There You Are: Mindfulness Meditation in Everyday Life*, says that meditation is about paying atten-

Books

In addition to the Jon Kabat-Zinn book mentioned earlier, you would be well served to read these:

- *Peace Is Every Step*, by Thich Nhat Hanh (Bantam Books, 1991).
- *Zen Mind, Beginner's Mind*, by Shunryu Suzuki (Weatherhill, 1988), a Zen master in Japan; these are transcripts from his lectures on a range of topics including the nuts and bolts of meditation.
- *Mindfulness in Plain English*, by Venerable Henepola Gunaratana (Wisdom Publications, 1993), who provides the fundamentals of vipassana meditation, which he says is "meant to revolutionize the whole of your life experience." You can actually read this online on several sites. Search by title on google.com.
- *A Path with Heart*, by Jack Kornfield (Bantam, 1993), who writes about integrating Eastern practices into our Western lives.

tion. It establishes a discipline in which you are intentional about being in the moment.

In meditation, you usually try to focus on something such as a word or sound. Probably the easiest thing to do is concentrate on your breathing, in and out, in and out. This will not be easy at first. "The mind has a life of its own," Jon says, "and it will wander." When that happens, you simply pull it back into focus on whatever you've chosen as a focus.

Concentrating on your breath may sound boring, but in his workshops, Jon suggests this exercise: Shut your mouth tight, grab your nose, and hold it. Then hold your breath as long as you can and notice how exquisitely beautiful the thought of taking a breath becomes.

An important thing to remember is that there is no right way to meditate, and if you concentrate too much on the question "Am I doing it right?" you won't be.

Meditation leads to mindfulness, to a deeper awareness of life and of the world, and an ability to live in the moment. This can become more important as we become older and realize more intensely how precious every moment is. It's also true that some of the most centered and grounded people I know meditate every day. They report that, in addition to the spiritual fulfillment, they require much less sleep and have more energy.

Many forms of meditation exist. Some examples include Vipassana, Transcendental, Christian, Zen, Buddhist, walking, and mindfulness.

Spiritual Retreats and Rituals

About seventeen years ago, I went to a weekend retreat near Santa Fe. This was a new experience for me in that I was just learning about religious and spiritual traditions. It was an extraordinary weekend, filled with great discussions late into the night, poetry readings, "smudging" rituals, music, and dancing.

One of the attendees was a Native American teacher and leader, Brooke Medicine Eagle, who had arranged to have a sweat lodge set up for anyone who was interested. I'd never heard of this before but since have learned that the ritual is focused on "purification, prayer, and healing," according to Josie RavenWing, author of *The Return of Spirit* and other books. "It takes place in what looks like a large inverted basket usually made of willow saplings and covered with blankets," Josie explains. "Stones that have been heated in a fire are brought into the lodge where water is poured on them, creating steam which helps to open the pores of the body and release toxins.

"The steam also carries the prayers and intentions of those gathered there and adds to the sacred space. All of life and all of creation is honored in the lodge, including our sacred ancestors. Everyone present is sitting, democratically and equally, on the earth. . . .

"It is dark within the lodge as within a womb, and this atmosphere encourages introspection, sometimes a dreamy state . . . and often a sense of deep connection with Nature. . . Many peoples or tribes had their own sweat lodge styles, including Native Americans and Irish."

My wife was intrigued and signed up for the sweat lodge; I opted for a poetry reading. I confess that the description of the ritual made the whole process sound, well, uncomfortable. But my wife said it was a transcendent experience for her, an altered state of consciousness.

I knew it to be true. Why? Because of what happened afterward. What I'm writing now is true and still remains in my memory as one of the most mysterious phenomena I've ever witnessed.

A group of us was gathered for an evening picnic along the river bank, with the sweat lodge people expected to arrive later. At some point, I looked up a hill to see my wife and the others coming from their sweat lodge experience. There are no adequate words to describe the energy between them. They were not talking, they were not holding hands, yet they were obviously connected.

But that was only half of it. I could see an aura of light around my wife as if she was glowing. The group along the river fell silent as we watched the sweat lodgers approach. Everyone saw the light; the effect was magic. I can't explain this and won't try, but I've always felt I missed something by not experiencing the lodge ritual.

In the intervening years, sweat lodges have become fairly common across the country, particularly among women. Apparently, for most people it is a life-changing and spiritually deepening experience. You need not go on a retreat to try it; you could do it in your backyard, for that matter. But you do need a ritual guide or at least someone who is willing to learn enough about it to act as guide. And please understand that this experience can serve to enhance your own spiritual insights regardless of your faith or philosophy.

Sometimes you can find out about people offering lodges in your area by asking around at various New Age or metaphyscial centers/bookstores. If there are Native American craft stores in your area, you might find someone there who knows and is willing to give you information.

You can, however, make your own structure, heat it with rocks, weave in the use of herbs such as laurel that is released into steam when water is poured on the hot rocks, and create a ritual of prayer and purification. These would more accurately be called "sweat baths." For more information on Native American sweats and sweat baths of all kinds from several traditions, check out **www.cyberbohemia.com/Pages/sweat.htm**.

If you decide to build one yourself, instructions and factors to consider are provided at **www.think-aboutit .com/native/building_a_sweat_lodge.htm**.

I HAVE BEEN astounded by the types and varieties of spiritual retreats available, from guided tours to holy sites and "power places," to holotrophic breathing weekends, to extended stays in monasteries and spiritual centers.

Whether you're Catholic, Protestant, Jewish, Buddhist, Hindu, Muslim, agnostic, or simply an interested skeptic, there's a place and an experience for you. You can go on active retreats in which you provide human services; you can go on fasting retreats and silence retreats;

you can find places to chant, sing, drum, dance, pray, or meditate.

But ask yourself some questions first. Start with purpose. Why do you think you want to do it? Do you need to sort out some things and refocus your life, are you trying to go deeper spiritually, or are you just curious? The answer to those questions leads to other questions about the kind of retreat that is most likely to accomplish your purpose.

Next, ask yourself whether you have the discipline to give yourself over to the process of the retreat. Can you sit silently and pray or meditate for hours? Can you go without conversation for days? Can you live without your evening glass of wine? Can you sleep on a hard bunk and eat simple and unexciting food? Part of the point of many retreats, particularly those in a monastic setting, is to give up the pleasures of the world in order to find something more fulfilling.

A retreat can be an important source of spiritual renewal, but it won't automatically solve all your problems.

Next, address your expectations realistically. Are you wanting to be "fixed" through this experience? Are you hoping for an epiphany? Do you expect to return to your life and everything will be all right? There are life problems that will yield to a retreat's emphasis on better focus and a more centered way of approaching

INTERNET RESOURCES: FINDING A RETREAT FOR YOU

You can find many resources for retreats through your place of worship and even through educational institutions. In addition, the following Web sites have large listings of possibilities:

www.SpiritSite.com lists a directory of spiritual retreat centers across the nation. These include Zen and yoga centers, residential spiritual communities, health spas (with a spiritual focus), desert ranches, and more.

www.Retreatsonline.com lists retreat getaways and locations and has descriptions of retreats in America, Canada, and international sites, in the following categories: *Nature/Activity*, which covers hiking and wilderness, houseboat, fishing, and farm retreats; *Travel/Destination*, including exotic locations and Journey to Sacred Lands Spiritual Retreats, which also includes yoga retreats; and *Health/Healing*, which offers fasting retreats. Contact Retreats Online, City Square PO Box 47105, Vancouver, Canada V5Z 4L6.

them, but some problems require other kinds of interior help such as psychotherapy or pastoral counseling. A retreat can be an important source of spiritual renewal, but it won't automatically solve all your problems.

Intentional Communities

For many people, perhaps most, the place of worship is the principal spiritual community in their lives, but worship services themselves rarely accommodate the need for a deep personal sharing by the congregants. Rather, depending on the faith or even denomination within a particular faith, a worship service is about people coming together to worship God according to prescribed rituals and practices. Even in the most unstructured Christian Protestant church services, there is generally still a printed order of worship.

This is not to deny that powerful spiritual experiences are possible within the context of regular worship services, nor is this to deny that intense personal connections exist among the congregants. This is only to contrast the worship community, often called the community of faith, from an intentional community of people who have chosen to come together "in community," to talk, to study, to meditate, to pray, or to engage in any practice that the community feels will bind them spiritually and will support their efforts to deepen or enlighten their mutual spiritual journey.

A general Web site about intentional communities, **www.ic.org,** features a list of intentional communities, an events calendar from *Communities* magazine, a way to reach other members of the group, and other resources for people interested in the concept of community. You can search the list alphabetically or by geographic location. Although this Web site sounds more hardworking and activist than reflective, communities are listed that resemble more of the kind of community I've just described.

Because of the personal nature of intentional communities, however, you might be better off talking with friends to form a community for agreed-upon reasons or placing an ad in your church bulletin or at another place where people with the same intention might gather.

There is no official rule book for intentional communities. There is no "right way" to create one. It requires only that the people involved agree among themselves as to why they are there and what they hope will evolve from the experience. The people can be friends or strangers. They can gather at a home or in a church basement or a meeting room anywhere.

A few practices seem common to such communities. Usually, the people sit in a circle with nothing in their laps—no note paper, no pens or pencils. There is no agenda. There are no leaders. One person may convene the gathering one time, another at another time. Or there may be no convenor at all.

Another common practice is to sit in silence for a while before talking. When talking begins, the people usually speak from their own experience, telling their own stories, concerns, needs, fears, joys, hopes, dreams. No one discusses politics or the world situation unless there is felt a pressing need for prayer or meditation about a particular situation (such as the Middle East).

Most of the community gatherings are quiet events, but I've known them to celebrate various holidays, birthdays, or other events with a ceremony or a potluck dinner. The point is that the people create and re-create this community according to their needs. You might say they make it up as they go along. The one consistent bonding principle is that they gather together because they want to support one another in the spiritual journey.

I was a member of an intentional community for two years. After that period, most of the members decided that it was time to pursue something else, to move on, always with the possibility that they would come together again in the future. Some of the members continued the community, which also is in contrast to regular worship services. The community may continue as long as the need is felt, which may be years, or it may be a periodic event.

In our community we convened once a week, usually in the evening. We sat silently for about twenty minutes, and then whoever felt moved to speak did so.

Many powerful moments and even some rather mystical happenings occurred. One evening before the meeting, we couldn't get one of the overhead lights to work. We tried new bulbs; we fiddled with the switch, checked the fuses. Nothing. We were left with only one overhead light.

Later, a couple were telling of their infant child who had died before ever leaving the hospital. It was an experience of overwhelming shared grief for all of us. We were grieved yet also comforted by the presence of others.

To close this phase of our gathering, we decided to sit silently and focus on the child who would never be in this world among us. Some called it prayer; others called it meditation; others called it sending energy into the universe. Those terminologies don't matter in an intentional community.

After a while, perhaps fifteen or twenty minutes, we opened our eyes and began to look around at one another. Suddenly the malfunctioning light came on brightly and burned the rest of the evening.

I'm sure someone somewhere would offer a perfectly rational explanation for the suddenly self-repaired light. A short, perhaps. A loose filament suddenly reconnecting. A dirty switch. Something rational and scientific, for sure.

But in the intentional community, we took it as a sign. Perhaps of life, or of reassurance about the great mystery of death. You can be sure that no one in the room searched for a technical explanation. And even if there was one, it would not in any way diminish for us the power or the importance of the incident.

Attitude as a Spiritual Practice

As I said at the beginning of this chapter, you don't have to participate in any kind of regular ritual or ceremony or group or activity in order to have a spiritual practice. While I've offered specific suggestions and ideas, the goal was not to urge you into one thing or another. The only real requirement is that you nurture an attitude of intentionality about living fully and deeply in the world, with open eyes, an open heart, and a sensitivity to others.

I think the true objective of any spiritual practice is not to let our own spiritual growth become an exclusive journey, an escape from the world, but instead to find the spiritual center of everyday life. And to help others find it. The practices in this chapter—indeed, the ideas and stories in this entire book—are about helping you in that journey as you come into the years of retirement.

The guiding questions should always revolve around the true reason for whatever disciplines you choose. Are they leading you to be as you want to be versus to do what you want to do? Can you find satisfaction with whatever you choose and with the "being" that it provides without having to wear your spiritual journey, your practice, or your service like a badge of honor, like another accomplishment? To put this another way, can you engage your spiritual life without feeling the need to build a "spiritual résumé?"

These are important questions for people who have spent a lifetime being measured and rewarded for doing and accomplishing things. Most of us fall into that category. But the concept of focusing on the being and not the doing of your life does not mean that you don't do anything. To the contrary, as the stories in this book make abundantly clear, the people who are most successful in getting done those things that help create their own personal journeys are also the people who know that the more they let go of goals and measurements in order to concentrate on the spiritual aspects of what they're engaged in, the more they get done.

As the Tao Te Ching points out about the person who is fully centered and grounded and who is able to manifest spirituality as part of everyday life: "When nothing is done, nothing is left undone."

Unless this sounds too easy, consider Jon Kabat-Zinn's observation that "Being is the hardest work on the planet."

Index